S0-AFH-721

Essential
Scotland

AAA Publishing 1000 AAA Drive, Heathrow, Florida 32746

Scotland: Regions and Best places to see

★ Best places to see 34–55 ■ Featured sight

D. M. HUNT LIBRARY
FALLS VILLAGE CONN

Original text by Hugh Taylor and Moira McCrossan
Revised and updated by Sally Roy

Edited, designed and produced by AA Publishing
© AA Media Limited 2010
Maps © AA Media Limited 2010

ISBN 978-1-59508-381-4

AA Media Limited retains the copyright in the original edition © 2000 and in all
subsequent editions, reprints and amendments.

All rights reserved. No part of this publication may be reproduced, stored in a
retrieval system, or transmitted in any form or by any means – electronic,
photocopying, recording or otherwise – unless the written permission of the
publishers has been obtained beforehand.

The contents of this publication are believed correct at the time of printing.
Nevertheless, the publishers cannot be held responsible for any errors or
omissions or for changes in the details given in this guide or for the
consequences of any reliance on the information provided by the same.

Published in the United States by AAA Publishing,
1000 AAA Drive, Heathrow, Florida 32746
Published in the United Kingdom by AA Publishing

Color separation: MRM Graphics Ltd
Printed and bound in Italy by Printer Trento S.r.l.

A04015

 This product includes mapping data licensed from Ordnance
Survey® with the permission of the Controller of Her
Majesty's Stationery Office. © Crown copyright 2010. All rights reserved. Licence
number 100021153

About this book

Symbols are used to denote the following categories:

➕ map reference to maps on cover

✉ address or location

☎ telephone number

🕐 opening times

✋ admission charge

🍴 restaurant or café on premises or nearby

Ⓜ nearest underground train station

🚌 nearest bus/tram route

🚉 nearest overground train station

⛴ nearest ferry stop

✈ nearest airport

❓ other practical information

ℹ tourist information office

▶ indicates the page where you will find a fuller description

This book is divided into five sections:

The essence of Scotland pages 6–19
Introduction; Features; Food and drink; Short break including the 10 Essentials

Planning pages 20–33
Before you go; Getting there; Getting around; Being there

Best places to see pages 34–55
The unmissable highlights of any visit to Scotland

Best things to do pages 56–71
Great places to have lunch; Stunning views; Places to take the children and more

Exploring pages 72–183
The best places to visit in Scotland organized by area

Maps
All map references are to the maps on the covers. For example, Inveraray has the reference ➕ 17H – indicating the grid square in which it is to be found

Admission prices
Inexpensive (under £4)
Moderate (£4–£7)
Expensive (over £7)

Hotel prices
Price are per room per night:
£ inexpensive (under £80)
££ moderate (£80–£150)
£££ expensive (over £150)

Restaurant prices
Price for a three-course meal per person without drinks:
£ inexpensive (under £20)
££ moderate (£20–£35)
£££ expensive (over £35)

Contents

D. M. HUNT LIBRARY
FALLS VILLAGE, CONN. 06031

The essence of. . .

THE ESSENCE OF SCOTLAND

Scots might have a reputation for thriftiness, but they're quick to share their country's pleasures. Whether you're casting for salmon on a crystal-clear river, tasting a single malt in a centuries-old distillery or tapping your toes to a Celtic reel in an inviting pub, it's a generosity you can't fail to appreciate.

Scotland has a depth and variety beyond its size. Edinburgh hosts a world-class festival but Scottish culture can be experienced across the land, from traditional Highland Games to the museums and art galleries of Glasgow. Scotland's unsurpassed landscape will win your heart, but it's her people, above all, that will provide some of the most indelible memories.

features

Trying to describe Scotland is like trying to capture the wind. When you think you've got it, it changes direction.

The central belt, industrialized and scarred yet displaying great beauty, includes the great cities of Edinburgh and Glasgow. The rolling hills and lush pastures of the South evoke emotions of a time long past, while in the Highlands there's a sense of wilderness created by the mountain ranges, the lochs and glens.

Scotland is also a land of history. Castles, towers and battlefields sit beside prehistoric stone monuments.

Then there are the people – descended from the Celts, integrating waves of Italian, Asian and Polish immigrants. The Scots take great delight in introducing visitors to their way of life. But take care, you might find you never want to go home.

GEOGRAPHY

The land area is 78,750sq km (30,405sq miles), much of it mountainous areas and islands. About 130 of Scotland's 800 islands are inhabited. The islands and the long sea lochs and estuaries create the 10,000km (6,215-mile) coastline. The Cairngorms is the largest area of peaks over 1,000m (3,280ft) in the UK and includes Ben Nevis, at 1,344m (4,408ft). There are about 30,000 lochs and 50,000km (30,000 miles) of river, which are among the least polluted in the world.

CLIMATE

The climate of Scotland in general is temperate but changeable. The Gulf Stream moderates temperatures in the west, while rain blows in from the Atlantic. The east tends to be cooler and drier. In the Highlands, snow is common in winter, often closing roads completely.

POPULATION

The population of Scotland is 5,200,000, most of which is concentrated in the central belt. Scotland is one of the least densely populated areas of Europe – around 66 people per sq km.

POLITICS AND SOCIETY

Scotland is divided into 32 local authorities. In 1999, the first Scottish parliament for 300 years took over domestic matters. Foreign policy and social security remain within the jurisdiction of the UK parliament.

CELTIC MUSIC

Celtic music is back in fashion and includes the music of the seven Celtic natioins – Scotland, Ireland, Wales, the Isle of Man, Cornwall, Brittany and Galicia – bound by a common thread but each unique. It is essentially a living tradition.

food & drink

Traditional Scottish cooking can be a culinary delight, but perseverance is required to find good examples. The poor diet of many Scots has dubbed Scotland the heart attack capital of Europe. Avoid the deep-fried Mars bar, but a fish supper (fish in batter with chips) can be good, especially in fishing areas.

FISH

As a fishing nation, the traditional food of the poor was tatties and herring (boiled potatoes with herring in oatmeal). The Arbroath smokie, whole haddock smoked in the traditional way, is the most refined smoked fish, delicious cooked with milk and butter. Avoid the vivid deep yellow of the chemically processed smoked haddock. Cullen skink, a soup made from smoked haddock, potatoes, onions and cream, is practically a meal in itself. Salmon is readily available since the increase in fish farming, but wild salmon can be found at good fishmongers. It may cost more but tastes superb.

MEAT

Haggis is the best-known Scottish meat dish, made from sheep offal, blood, spices and oatmeal and boiled in a sheep's stomach, and traditionally eaten with mashed tatties (potatoes) and neeps (turnips). Scottish Aberdeen Angus beef and fine flavoured hill lamb are superb, and don't miss the chance to try venison from the wild red deer or local game such as grouse or pheasant. The traditional dish for New Year is steak pie. Good butchers make their own steak pies, which have flaky pastry and a rich gravy, and mutton pies with thin pastry filled with minced meat.

SCOTTISH MEALS

A traditional Scottish breakfast starts with porridge, followed by eggs, bacon, square slice (a kind of beef sausage), black pudding (a spicy blood pudding), potato scones and tomatoes. This comes with copious quantities of tea, buttered rolls and marmalade. If you need lunch after this, pick up a midday snack of Scotch Broth or pie and beans in a pub or café.

For eating out in the evening, there are many excellent restaurants specializing in traditional and imaginative Scottish menus. A typical menu might start with smoked salmon or partan bree (crab soup), serve high-quality Aberdeen Angus or game as a main course and finish off with the luxurious cranachan, a dish which combines toasted oatmeal with raspberries, cream, honey and whisky. Before or after dessert, local cheeses such as Dunsyre Blue or Dunlop might be served with oatcakes.

Traditionally, fine food is accompanied by French wine but to round off the evening try Drambuie, a whisky-based liqueur made from a secret recipe originating with Bonnie Prince Charlie.

THE NATIONAL DRINK

Whisky, Scotland's national drink, is distilled from barley. There are hundreds of malt whiskies, aged for 10 or 12 years, sometimes more, in wooden casks. The taste of each malt reflects the spring water, the peat, the type of cask and the years of maturation. Most pubs have a selection of the better-known malts.

Advertised as 'Scotland's other national drink', Irn-Bru is an orange-coloured non-alcoholic fizzy drink, reputed to cure hangovers. There could be no other reason for drinking it.

OATS

Oatmeal is a staple Scottish ingredient. Porridge, made by cooking oatmeal in water or milk, is eaten salted, sometimes

with cream, never with sugar. In times past, cooked porridge would be poured into the bottom drawer of a dresser, then cut into slices and eaten cold. Oatcakes are made from oatmeal flour and butter. Try to find ones made by the dozens of small local producers, who often make delicious variations.

SWEET TOOTH

Cakes and sweets are popular in Scotland. Most well known are the traditional Dundee cake, a rich fruit concoction decorated with almonds; and shortbread, a thick biscuit made from flour, butter and sugar. The Scotch pancake – a small drop scone eaten hot or cold with butter and syrup or jam – is also a firm favourite. Don't miss tablet, the delicious butterscotch candy made

from sugar, water and butter; and Edinburgh rock, a crumbly sweet made into sticks flavoured with vanilla, ginger or lemon.

short break

If you only have a short time to visit Scotland, or would like to get a really complete picture of the country, here are the essentials:

● **Sample malt whisky.** There are so many varieties to choose from, but try the peaty taste of Islay Bowmore and the smooth, almost velvet quality of Grants Balvenie.

● **Visit Glasgow's Barras.** Listen to the patter of the vendors at this famous weekend flea market in the east end.

- **Visit the National Museum of Scotland.** Opened in January 1999, the museum tells Scotland's story from the geological creation of the land to 20th-century industry (➤ 79.

- **Go to a pub music session.** The finest traditional Scottish music is found in informal pub sessions. Try Sandy Bell's Bar in Edinburgh (➤ 70).

- **Eat haggis, neeps and tatties.** Scotland's national dish is on the menu in many pubs and restaurants. Wash it down with a wee dram of whisky.

● **Head for the coast.** Whether it's the east, west or north, Scotland's coast offers scenic beauty in huge variety – often with fabulous views to the offshore islands.

● **Go to a village gala.** Most small villages have a gala day with street parades, crowning of the Gala Queen, outdoor activities and a ceilidh (traditional Gaelic dance) in the village hall.

● **Visit one of the great abbey ruins in the South.** Some of the most atmospheric are Jedburgh (➤ 85) and Melrose (➤ 87) in the Borders or Dundrennan and Sweetheart (➤ 115) in Dumfries and Galloway.

● **Visit Edinburgh Castle.** If you only see one thing, it has to be this (➤ 42–43). Then walk down the historic Royal Mile to the Palace of Holyroodhouse (➤ 79) and the Scottish Parliament (➤ 82).

● **Ride the train from Inverness to Kyle of Lochalsh.** It's one of the most scenic rail routes in Britain, particularly when viewed from the special observation cars.

Planning

Before you go

WHEN TO GO

JAN	FEB	MAR	APR	MAY	JUN	JUL	AUG	SEP	OCT	NOV	DEC
5°C	5°C	8°C	11°C	14°C	16°C	18°C	18°C	15°C	11°C	9°C	7°C
41°F	41°F	46°F	52°F	57°F	61°F	64°F	64°F	59°F	52°F	48°F	45°F

High season   Low season

With the sea and ocean on three sides, Scotland's climate is nothing if not unpredictable. Seasonal variations in temperature and rainfall differ regionally. The highlands of the Cairngorms can suffer blizzards in late spring while areas of the west coast, warmed by the Gulf Stream, can be mild enough for tropical plants. Late spring (May–Jun) tends to be drier than the middle of the summer (Jul–Aug) and the east coast tends to have less rainfall than the west. Temperatures are variable, but July and August are usually the hottest months with average temperatures of up to 20°C (68°F). One seasonal feature to consider is the hatching of the midges, tiny biting insects prevalent in some rural areas. The midges appear in June and don't die out until the cooler weather of September. The west of Scotland suffers greater midge outbreaks than the east.

WHAT YOU NEED

● Required
○ Suggested
▲ Not required

Some countries require a passport to remain valid for a minimum period (usually at least six months) beyond the date of entry – check before you travel.

	UK	Germany	USA	Netherlands	Spain
Passport	▲	●	●	●	●
Visa (Regulations can change – check before booking your journey)	▲	▲	▲	▲	▲
Onward or Return Ticket	▲	○	○	○	○
Health Inoculations	▲	▲	▲	▲	▲
Health Documentation (➤ 23, Health Insurance)	▲	●	●	●	●
Travel Insurance	○	○	○	○	○
Driving Licence (national)	●	●	●	●	●
Car Insurance Certificate (if own car)	▲	●	●	●	●
Car Registration Document (if own car)	▲	●	●	●	●

WEBSITES

www.visithighlands.com
www.edinburgh.org
www.seeglasgow.com

www.scot-borders.co.uk
www.nts.org.uk
www.historic-scotland.gov.uk

TOURIST OFFICES AT HOME

In Scotland

Ocean Point One
94 Ocean Drive, Leith
Edinburgh EH6 6JH
☎ 0131 332 2433
www.visitscotland.com

In the USA

British Tourist Authority
551 Fifth Avenue, 7th Floor,
Suite 701, New York, NY 10176-0799
☎ 800/462 2748
www.cometoscotland.com

In England

Scottish Tourist Board
19 Cockspur Street
London SW1 5BL
☎ 020 7930 2812

HEALTH INSURANCE

Nationals of the EU and certain other countries receive reduced cost
emergency medical treatment in the UK with the relevant documentation,
although private medical insurance is still advised and is essential for all
other visitors. Dental treatment is very limited under the National Health
Service scheme and even EU nationals will probably have to pay.
However, private medical insurance will cover you.

TIME DIFFERENCES

GMT	Scotland	Germany	USA (NY)	Netherlands	Spain
12 noon	12 noon	1PM	7AM	1PM	1PM

Scotland, like the rest of the UK, is on Greenwich Mean Time. The clocks
are advanced by one hour in the spring and brought back one hour in the
autumn. Continental Europe is always at least one hour ahead.

NATIONAL HOLIDAYS

Scottish public holidays may vary from place to place and their dates from year to year, so although the capital Edinburgh may be on holiday at certain times, other Scottish towns and cities will not necessarily be having a public holiday. Major holidays throughout the country are:

1 Jan *New Year's Day*
2 Jan *Bank Holiday*
Mar/Apr *Good Friday/Easter Monday*
First Mon May *May Day*
Bank Holiday
Last Mon May *Spring Bank Holiday*
Last Mon Aug *August Bank Holiday*
Mon nearest 30 Nov *St Andrew's Day*
25 Dec *Christmas Day*
26 Dec *Boxing Day*

WHAT'S ON WHEN

January *The Ba'*, Orkney: Very dangerous game of street soccer between two teams, the Uppies and the Downies, played through the streets of Kirkwall, seemingly with few rules.

Celtic Connections, Royal Concert Hall, Glasgow: Three weeks of music and culture.

Up Helly Aa, Lerwick, Shetland: Annual Viking Fire Festival which takes place on the last Tuesday in January irrespective of the weather.

Robert Burns Night: On the anniversary of the poet's birthday (25 January) people gather for a traditional Burns Supper of haggis, neeps and tatties, a few drams of whisky, and poetry and song.

February *Scottish Curling Championship:* Grown men and women hurl lumps of rock along ice.

March *Whuppity Stoorie*, Lanark: Winter is symbolically banished by children running round the church hitting each other with paper weapons.

April *The Scottish Grand National*, Ayr Racecourse.

Edinburgh International Folk Festival.

May *Girvan Traditional Folk Festival:* A picturesque fishing harbour, intimate concert venues with top performers and unbelievable pub sessions combine to make this the best small folk festival in Scotland.

Loch Shiel Festival: Classical music in the Highlands

Beltane Fire Festival, Calton Hill, Edinburgh: On 1 May, an ancient Pagan festival to celebrate the coming of spring.

June *Riding the Marches*, various Border towns: Traditionally to check the boundaries of the common land.

July *World Flounder Tramping Championships,* Palnackie, Dumfriesshire: When the little fish tickle your feet you realize this event is not as easy as it sounds.

Moniaive Gala: Picturesque Dumfriesshire village at its best. Procession followed by a fair, and in the evening a ceilidh dance.

August *Edinburgh Arts Festival, Fringe and Military Tattoo.*

September *Braemar Highland Games:* Games take place across Scotland, but this is the one to see.

October *The National Mod:* Gaeldom's competition showcase. A different Highland town is chosen as the venue each year.

30 November *St Andrew's Day.*

31 December *Hogmanay:* Seeing the old year out and the new one in. Traditional first-footing – visiting neighbours and friends with a bottle and something to eat – is dying out. Instead, parties are the trend with Edinburgh's Princes Street Gardens the venue for the world's largest.

Getting there

BY AIR

Glasgow Airport		
━━━━━━▶●	🚇	N/A
	🚌	20 minutes
14 kilometres (9 miles) to city centre	🚗	15 minutes

Edinburgh Airport		
━━━━━━▶●	🚇	N/A minutes
	🚌	25 minutes
14 kilometres (9 miles) to city centre	🚗	25 minutes

Scotland has four main international airports – Glasgow, Edinburgh, Aberdeen and Prestwick. Scheduled and charter flights arrive daily at all of them from Europe, USA and the rest of the UK. There are direct flights to Glasgow from North America.

EDINBURGH

Edinburgh's airport (www.edinburghairport.com) is to the west of the city.

Public transport There is no rail link between the airport, to the west of the city centre on the ring road, and central Edinburgh. However, a public bus service, the Airlink 100, runs from the Arrivals exit at the airport to Waverley Bridge in central Edinburgh every 10 minutes from 4:45am to past midnight. Tickets cost £3.50 one-way and £6 round-trip and can be purchased in the Arrivals hall or on the bus (☎ 0131 555 6363; www.flybybus.com).

The Edinburgh Shuttle (☎ 0845 500 5000; www.edinburghshuttle.com) offers shared minibuses to destinations within the city centre (including hotels and private homes). The service departs every 15–30 minutes and costs £9 each way.

Taxi There are three taxi stands at the airport, with private hire vehicles operating from the east end of the terminal and black cabs departing from the same area. The third rank is on the ground floor of the short-stay car park. Travel time into the city is about 25 minutes; allow longer during the rush hour. Many taxis are wheelchair accessible.

Car To drive from the airport to Edinburgh, take the eastbound A8, which leads to the centre. Alternatively, follow the A8 west until the M9 intersection; the M9 heads to Stirling while the M8 goes to Glasgow.

GLASGOW

Glasgow's airport (www.glasgowairport.com) is just off the M8 motorway.
Public transport The nearest rail station is Paisley's Gilmour Street station, 2km (1 mile) from the airport. A taxi or bus (numbers 66 or 300) will drop you at the station. From Gilmour Street there is a frequent service to Glasgow Central station (between 5 and 8 trains an hour). Buses for the city centre depart from the Departures exit. Choose from: the Glasgow Flyer (every 10 minutes; journey time 15–25 minutes; single £4.20, return £6.20); Airlink Direct 757 (every 20 minutes; journey time 25 minutes; single £2.90, return £5) or the 747 Airlink Cityservice (every 30 minutes; journey time 50 minutes; single £2.90, single plus city travel for one week £13.50), which travels via Renfrew to Buchanan bus station.
Taxi and car A taxi stand outside the terminal building has taxis available 24 hours a day. Drivers should take the M8 motorway into the centre.

Getting around

PUBLIC TRANSPORT
Internal flights British Airways (☎ 0844 4930 787;
www.britishairways.com) has scheduled flights linking the main cities and
provides a service to the islands, including Orkney and Shetland.

Trains Most of Scotland's rail service is operated by First Scotrail (☎ 0845
7550 033; www.scotrail.co.uk). GNER (☎ 0845 7225 111;
www.gnertickets.co.uk) and Virgin (☎ 0845 7222 333;
www.virgintrains.co.uk) also operate services.

Long-distance buses Scottish Citylink (☎ 0870 5505 050;
www.citylink.co.uk) covers most of the country as well as linking to the
rest of the UK. Local companies provide connecting services to areas not
covered by Citylink and in the Highlands, Islands and remote rural areas
there are Post Buses run by the Royal Mail (☎ 0845 7740 740).

Ferries Caledonian MacBrayne (☎ 0870 5650 000; www.calmac.co.uk)
covers the main island destinations on the West Coast including the
Western Islands. For Orkney and Shetland, Northlink Ferries (☎ 0845
6000 449; www.northlinkferries.co.uk)
sails from Aberdeen and Scrabster.

Urban transport In the main towns
and cities the public transport network
is fairly extensive. Glasgow has
Scotland's only underground and is
also well served by urban trains and
buses. Elsewhere a plethora of bus
companies compete for passengers.

FARES AND TICKETS
Tickets are often cheaper if purchased in advance. Some forms of
transport are more expensive at peak times; planes and trains especially
so. Off-peak periods tend to start after 9:15am and include weekends.

TAXIS

In cities and larger towns the standard black hackney cabs are licensed, have meters and should display rates. Minicabs and private rental cars will also be licensed and may be metered. If

not, agree on a fare before entering the vehicle.

DRIVING

- Speed limit on motorways and two-way highways 112kph (70mph).
- Speed limit outside built-up areas 96kph (60mph).
- Speed limits in built-up areas 48kph (30mph), unless varied by signs.
- Seat belts must be worn in front and rear seats at all times.
- Random breath-testing. Never drive under the influence of alcohol.
- Fuel (petrol) is expensive and available in two grades: Unleaded and Super Unleaded, in addition to diesel. Prices vary and it is much more expensive in the Highlands and Islands. The least expensive fuel is sold at supermarkets with filling stations. Opening hours are variable with some 24-hour stations on motorways (highways) and large urban areas.
- SOS telephones are located at regular intervals along motorways (highways). Roadside assistance operated by the Automobile Association (☎ 0800 88 77 66; www.theaa.com) has a 24-hour breakdown service for members and for members of organizations with reciprocal agreements.

CAR RENTAL

Most major companies have facilities at airports, major towns and cities. Reserving in advance can avoid lengthy waits at peak periods. Avis (☎ 0844 5810 147; www.avis.co.uk). Budget (☎ 0844 5819 998; www.budget.co.uk). Thrifty (☎ 01494 751 500; www.thrifty.co.uk).

Being there

TOURIST OFFICES

Edinburgh and Lothians
3 Princes Street (above Waverley
Station), Edinburgh
☎ 0131 473 3800
www.edinburgh.org

**Greater Glasgow and the
Clyde Valley**
11 George Square, Glasgow
☎ 0141 566 0800
www.seeglasgow.com

Highlands and Islands
Castle Wynd, Inverness
☎ 01845 2255 121
www.visithighlands.com

Aberdeen and Grampian
Exchange House
27 Albyn Place, Aberdeen
☎ 01224 288828
www.aberdeenhq.com

Dumfries and Galloway
64 Whitesands, Dumfries
☎ 01387 253862
www.dumfriesandgalloway.co.uk

Shetland
Market Cross
Lerwick, Shetland
☎ 01595 999440
www.visitshetland.com

MONEY

The British unit of currency is the pound sterling, divided into 100p
(pence). Its symbol, placed before the pounds, is £. There are coins for
1p and 2p (copper), 5p, 10p, 20p and 50p (silver), £1 (gold-colour), £2
(silver and gold-colour); and bank notes for £5, £10, £20, £50 and £100.
Scottish banks issue their own notes including £1 banknotes. Scottish
banknotes are acceptable, though may be unfamiliar, throughout the UK.

TIPS/GRATUITIES

Yes ✓ No ✗

Restaurants (if service not included)	✓	10%
Cafés/bars (if service not included)	✓	10%
Hairdressers	✓	£1–£2
Taxis	✓	10%
Cloakroom attendants	✓	£1
Porters/Chambermaids	✓	£1 a bag/£2
Toilet attendants	✗	

POSTAL SERVICES

Each town and most large villages have at least one post office. Opening hours are 9–5:30 Mon–Fri and 9–12:30 Sat, closed Sun. Small offices close for lunch from 1pm to 2pm. Stamps are also sold by some newspaper shops and shops selling postcards.

INTERNET

High-speed internet access is widely available in cities and larger towns although don't expect it in the more remote areas. While some hotels may offer free internet access it is more usual to be charged. Wireless broadband is increasingly available in hotels and city centre coffee shops.

TELEPHONES

Public telephones on the street and in bars, hotels and restaurants accept 10p, 20p, 50p, £1 and £2 coins, while others can only be used with phone cards (available from newspaper shops and post offices). Costs are considerably less expensive than using the phone in your hotel room.

International dialling codes

From the UK to:

France: 00 33
Germany: 00 49

Spain: 00 34
USA: 00 1
Netherlands: 00 31

Emergency telephone number

Police, Fire, Ambulance: 999

CONSULATES AND HIGH COMMISSIONS (EDINBURGH)

USA ☎ 0131 556 8315
Germany ☎ 0131 337 2323

Netherlands ☎ 0131 220 3226
Spain ☎ 0131 220 1843

HEALTH ADVICE

Sun advice It is possible to get sunburn and sunstroke, particularly during the summer. Avoid prolonged exposure and use sunblock or cover up.

Drugs Prescription, non-prescription drugs and medicines are available from pharmacies. Non-prescription drugs and medicines are also widely available in supermarkets.

Safe water Tap water is generally safe to drink.

PERSONAL SAFETY

Theft from cars is unfortunately common, as are the usual crimes associated with big cities such as bag snatching and pickpockets. Any crime should be reported to the police and a report requested if you plan to file an insurance claim.

- Never leave anything of value in your car. Place all bags out of sight.
- Keep passports, tickets and valuables in a hotel safe deposit box.
- Avoid wearing a camera around your neck or displaying valuables.
- Wear your bag across your chest rather than over your shoulder.
- Don't walk alone in dimly lit areas at night.

ELECTRICITY

The electricity supply is 240 volts. Sockets take square three pin plugs. All visitors from other countries will require an adaptor. American appliances also require a voltage converter.

OPENING HOURS

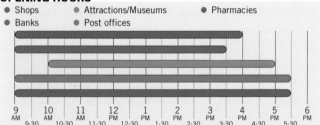

The above times are general and there are variations. Shops will usually remain open throughout lunch and even on Sundays in the larger towns, cities and tourist resorts. Supermarkets will also be open seven days and close between 7pm and 10pm but several now offer 24-hour opening Monday to Friday, mainly in the cities. Markets are generally open 8–4. In rural areas shops will close for an hour at lunch time, generally 1–2pm, for one afternoon each week and all day Sunday.

LANGUAGE

The language of the country is English but even English-speaking people may have some difficulties with the Scots language when specifically Scots words are used. These will vary according to region. In Aberdeen the dialect is known as Doric, in the Lowlands of Scotland it is Lallans, the city of Glasgow has a patter all of its own and in Orkney and Shetland the local dialect has Scandinavian roots. Although you may not wish to use the dialects, knowing the most common dialect words will ease understanding.

ashet a large serving dish

bannock a round flat cake cooked on a griddle

brose a type of porridge made from oats or pease-meal

bridie a spicy meat and onion pasty

butterie or **rowie** a croissant-like bread roll with lots of butter

caller fresh

clootie dumpling a rich fruit cake, boiled in a cloth

aye yes

naw no

ceilidh dance or party

greet to cry

bairn, chiel, wean child

hen, quine, wifie, lassie girl or woman

jimmy, loon, laddie man or boy

brae hill

burn a stream

glen valley

braw good

dreich overcast and dull

droukit soaked

glaur mud

dram a measure of whisky

drouth thirst

drouthy thirsty

gigot or **shank** a leg of lamb or pork; gigot is normally the thick end and shank the thin end

haggis dish made from offal, blood, oatmeal and spices, boiled in a sheep's stomach

tatties potatoes

champit tatties mashed potatoes

haiver to talk rubbish

ken to know

kenspeckle well known

muckle big

blether to gossip

crabbit bad-tempered

nyaff, scunner unpleasant person

greetin'-faced miserable person

kirk church

cairn a pile of stones used as a marker or memorial

gloaming evening

simmer dim mid-summer when it never gets quite dark but the sun just dips below the horizon

tattie scones flat scone made of potatoes and flour

tattie bogle scarecrow

stovies potatoes cooked with onion and a little meat

piece sandwich

play piece playtime snack

jeelie piece jam sandwich

piece break mid-morning break

girdle gridle or flat iron plate for cooking scones on top of the stove

messages shopping, normally for groceries

speir ask or enquire

stravaig to wander abroad

peelie wallie pale and wan

shilpit thin

sleekit sly

sonsie healthy looking

thrawn perverse

furth outside the area

sooth south; in Orkney and Shetland refers to the mainland

smirr just a little rain in the air

snell cold

stoating bouncing; used when describing heavy rain

Best places to see

1 Burns National Heritage Park

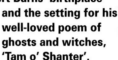

www.burnsheritagepark.com

Alloway was Robert Burns' birthplace and the setting for his well-loved poem of ghosts and witches, 'Tam o' Shanter'.

Robert Burns' father, William Burnes, built his 'auld clay biggin' near the banks of the River Doon, with walls 1m (3ft) thick and tiny windows to protect against the chill Scottish winters. This long, low, thatched cottage, where Robert was born, still stands today at the heart of the Burns National Heritage Park. Among the fascinating memorabilia on display in the adjacent museum are a plaster cast of the poet's skull, his Bible, and various original manuscripts, including the world's most famous song of parting, 'Auld Lang Syne'.

The manuscript of 'Tam o' Shanter', also on view in the museum, is translated into virtual reality at the nearby visitor centre in the Tam o' Shanter Experience. This hilarious and atmospheric tale recounts how the hapless Tam, in a drunken stupor, blunders upon the witches, then entranced by the pretty young Nannie, roars out, 'Weel done Cutty sark!', only to be chased from Alloway Kirk to the Brig o' Doon by a 'hellish legion' of witches. The reality of 'Alloway's auld haunted kirk' is nearby and in this eerie ruin it is easy to imagine the open coffins and malignant tokens of the poem. Follow the chase from here to the Brig o' Doon, where Tam's mare Meg lost her tail to the winsome witch. This narrow old stone bridge was on the main road from Ayr to Carrick, a route well trodden by Burns. The site is owned by the National Trust for Scotland, and work started in 2009 on a major redevelopment plan.

🕂 17K ✉ Murdoch's Lone, Alloway ☎ 01292 443700
🕒 Apr–Sep daily 10–5:30; Oct–Mar 10–5
✋ Moderate 🍴 Tea room (Jun–Sep) (£) 🚌 Western 57 from Ayr to Alloway, hourly
🚊 Nearest train station Ayr

SACRED
TO THE MEMORY OF
William Burns
FARMER IN LOCHLIE,
who died on the 13th Feb 1784,
in the 65d year of his age.
AND OF
Agnes Brown
HIS SPOUSE,
who died on the 19th Jan 1820,
in the 88 year of her age.

2 Burrell Collection

www.glasgowmuseums.com

This wonderful museum is built around an exquisite, idiosyncratic collection, gathered over a period of 80 years.

The millionaire shipping magnate Sir William Burrell left his eclectic collection of paintings, tapestries, stained glass, furniture, silver and precious objects to the people of Glasgow in 1944. He was a magpie who started collecting as a boy and continued until his death in 1958, by which time his acquisitions numbered some 8,000 treasures and objects from around the world.

For years the collection lay in storerooms until the present building, specifically designed around the concept of displaying the collection to its best advantage, was constructed in 1983. This red sandstone, wood and glass structure nestles in a corner of the parkland next to a grove of chestnut and sycamore. Inside, the great glass walls bring the woodlands into the heart of the museum. Medieval stone doorways and windows have been built into the fabric of the building, antique stained glass hangs before the glass walls and the rooms are clad in ancient tapestries. Three rooms from Burrell's home at Hutton Castle have been re-created with their windows looking out on to the glass-roofed central courtyard. The collection is strong on rare oriental porcelain and fine medieval French tapestries, but also includes work by Cézanne, Degas and Rodin. It is intriguing not just for the objects and the building but because of the man who assembled it.

✚ *Glasgow 1d (off map)* ✉ Pollok Country Park, Glasgow
☎ 0141 287 2550 ⏰ Mon–Thu, Sat, 10–5, Fri, Sun 11–5
✋ Free 🍴 Café (£) 🚌 45, 47, 48, 57 from central Glasgow
🚇 Pollokshaws West, then 10 minutes' walk

3 Culloden Battlefield

www.nts.org.uk

This desolate moor, where the last battle on British soil was fought, was the scene of savage slaughter after the defeat of the Jacobites.

This bleak moorland has been restored to the condition it was in on that fateful morning in 1746 when the hopes of the Royal House of Stuart to regain the throne of Scotland were forever dashed. It is a melancholy site where, tradition has it, the birds never sing and where no heather grows on the graves of the clansmen slaughtered in the aftermath by the forces of the Duke of Cumberland.

The broad, windswept expanse of Culloden Moor was ideal for the government's cavalry and artillery – the entrenched guns laid waste the Highland ranks. When finally the Highlanders charged, they became bogged down in the mud and scattered in disorder. Their infantry, already outnumbered, exhausted and starving after the long march from Derby, faltered and fell under a murderous hail of shot. The wounded survivors were slaughtered where they lay, and indiscriminate butchery of men, women and children was encouraged by Cumberland on the road to Inverness. The following year, all weapons, bagpipes, tartan and the kilt were banned by law in a bid to destroy the Highland culture and the clan system. Today, the episode is described in an excellent audiovisual display in the visitor centre, while state-of-the art audio handsets will guide you round the battlefield itself.

The Battle of Culloden was the last battle of the Jacobite rebellion of 1745, and the final defeat was followed by cruelty and years of persecution. An oppressive sadness and poignancy surrounds the memorial cairns, the sort of atmosphere that clings to such places as the Somme and Auschwitz which have witnessed pitiless waste of human life.

✚ 8D ✉ 10km (6 miles) east of Inverness ☎ 01463 790607 🕐 Battlefield always open. Visitor Centre: Apr–Oct daily 9–6; Nov–Mar 10–4. Closed Christmas, 1–2 and 10–29 Jan ✋ Moderate 🍴 Restaurant 'Tastes of Scotland' (£–££) 🚌 Rapson's No 7 bus from Inverness

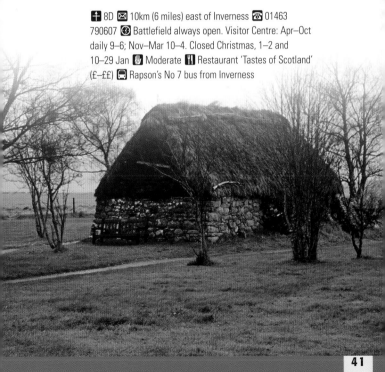

4 Edinburgh Castle

www.edinburghcastle.gov.uk

Home to monarchs, scene of banquets and siege, this castle is not only at the heart of Scotland's capital but of its history.

Edinburgh Castle dominates the city from every angle and is visible from miles away. Over a million people visit every year and the queues for the Crown Room start to form early every day. The ancient Honours of Scotland are the oldest crown jewels in Europe, and the Stone of Destiny on which all Scots monarchs were crowned is also on display here.

There's been a fortification on this great volcanic rock since Celtic times, and the tiny Norman St Margaret's Chapel, the oldest building in Edinburgh, has stood intact for more than 900 years. The Royal Apartments include the room where Mary, Queen of Scots gave birth to the future James VI of Scotland (James I of England). The Great Hall has seen many historic gatherings and is still used for receptions by the Scottish First Minister. In the castle's cellar is the colossal cannon called Mons Meg, which fired its massive stone cannonballs at the Battle of Flodden in 1513, a devastating defeat for the Scots by the English. At 1pm you can witness the firing of the one o'clock gun – not Mons Meg! The custom, which dates

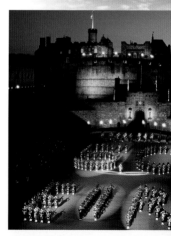

back to an era when few people owned clocks or watches, distinguishes the residents from the visitors. Visitors are often startled, Edinburgh folk just check their watches.

In August, the Castle Esplanade is the venue for the world-famous Edinburgh Military Tattoo. For three weeks the Army presents a dramatic, floodlit programme of music, marching and historical re-enactments. Almost as impressive as the castle itself are the views of the city of Edinburgh and surrounding countryside from its ramparts.

✚ *Edinburgh 2c* ✉ Castlehill ☎ 0131 225 9846
🕐 Apr–Oct daily 9:30–6; Nov–Mar 9:30–5 ✋ Expensive
🍴 Cafés (£–££) 🚉 Waverley

5 Glen Coe

This majestic mountain pass running from Glencoe village to Rannoch Moor is one of the most spectacular and dramatic sights in Scotland.

Lying at the foot of massive mountains, often disappearing into heavy swirling cloud, the gloom in Glen Coe can be oppressive. Under clear blue skies, the smooth green humps of the mountains, the rocky summits of the Three Sisters, the wide floor of the glen and the distant mountain tops beyond are a familiar sight the world over on calendars and in films. *Braveheart*, *Restless Natives*, *Highlander* and many other movies were shot in the Glen.

There is an awesome stillness about the Glen, which even the great numbers of tourists, walkers and climbers never disturb. However, its peace was rudely shattered on a winter morning more than 300 years ago when Glen Coe became a byword

for treachery. The chief of the Clan MacDonald was late in swearing allegiance to the Crown. Campbell of Glenlyon, under orders signed by King William, took his men to Glencoe to make an example of the MacDonalds. He billeted his men there on the pretext that they were just passing through. In the early dawn of 13 February, 1692, throughout the glen, the Campbells dragged MacDonald men from their beds and murdered them, burning the houses as they went. The women, some carrying infants, fled into the mountains in a piercing snowstorm, many perishing miserably.

Nowadays the unpredictable weather still claims lives among the skiers, walkers and climbers who flock to the Glen. There are countless challenging walks and climbs, but this is no land for a casual afternoon stroll.

In summer a trip up the ski lift to the summit will be rewarded by spectacular views over Rannoch Moor and the surrounding mountains.

➕ 6F ✉ 24km (15 miles) south of Fort William
🍴 Snack bar in Glencoe Village (£) 🚌 Scottish City Link
   from Glasgow and Fort William

6 New Lanark

www.newlanark.org.uk

New Lanark was the first example of a working environment planned to consider the welfare of the workforce as well as efficiency and profit.

Designated a World Heritage Site in 2001, this was Robert Owen's utopian village, built near the Falls of Clyde to harness the power of the water for driving the cotton mills. New Lanark was much more than a mill town; it was a model village, and Owen (1771–1858) was the forerunner of the great Victorian philanthropists who built towns such as Saltaire and Port Sunlight. Contrary to the wisdom of the time, Owen believed that a happy workforce would be a productive workforce, so he provided modern housing, a shop, a school and recreation facilities. His employees also worked shorter hours and had better working conditions, schooling was compulsory and he did not employ children under 10 in the mill.

His competitors thought he was crazy and that his business would suffer. They were astonished when it became even more profitable. New Lanark survived as a mill town

into the 20th century and was saved from ultimate demolition when it was restored as a conservation project. You can tour the houses, gardens and recreation hall, see the restored looms working and learn about life at the time through the eyes of a young girl in the Annie McLeod Experience.

Although it is in the industrial heartland of Scotland, New Lanark is set in a rural location by the Clyde. This was part of Owen's plan that his workers should live in pleasant surroundings. You can follow the delightful riverside walk to the Falls of Clyde to appreciate the importance of this.

✚ 19K ✉ New Lanark World Heritage Site ☎ 01555 665738 🕔 Apr–Sep daily 10:30–5; Nov–Mar 11–5 ✋ Moderate 🍴 Tea room (£) 🚌 Bus service from station in Lanark 🚆 Lanark
ℹ Horsemarket, Ladyacre Road, Lanark ☎ 01555 661661

7 Rosslyn Chapel

www.rosslynchapel.org.uk

This tiny, atmospheric medieval chapel is an exquisite masterpiece of the mason's art, with an unrivalled range and delicacy of carving.

Rosslyn Chapel is possibly the most mysterious building in Scotland, like a great medieval cathedral in miniature. It is richly carved, including the most complete *danse macabre* (dance of death) in Europe and the death mask of King Robert the Bruce, reproduced in stone. Built by Sir William St Clair, it has strong connections with the Knights Templar, a mystical order of wealthy warrior monks, who fought with Robert the Bruce at Bannockburn (1314). They were credited with finding the Holy Grail and the treasures of Solomon.

It is said that the Holy Grail is hidden in the Apprentice Pillar, one of two great pillars. The story goes that the apprentice saw the pillar in a dream and carved it in his master's absence. The master

was so jealous when he saw the delicate and complicated work that he felled the apprentice with a single blow of his mallet. The master was hanged, and his effigy and that of the apprentice and his mother can be found close to the pillars. Whatever the truth, there is no doubt that the master masons who chiselled these intricate patterns and medieval likenesses were exceptionally gifted.

Whether it is the medieval faces peering out of the stone on all sides or the 20 knights in full armour interred below, there is a supernatural feel to this tiny chapel and a strange chill as you enter the crypt. The chapel has found recent fame through its connection with the best-selling novel *The Da Vinci Code* by Dan Brown.

✚ 20J ✉ Off Chapel Loan, Roslin (11km/7 miles south of Edinburgh) ☎ 0131 440 2159 🕐 Apr–Sep Mon–Sat 9:30–6; Oct–Mar Mon–Sat 9:30–5; Sun 12–4:45 all year ✋ Expensive 🍴 Coffee shop (£) 🚌 15 (Lothian) from Edinburgh

8 Skara Brae

www.historic-scotland.gov.uk

On a beautiful sandy seashore on the edge of the world is the perfectly preserved neolithic settlement of Skara Brae in Orkney.

Buried for centuries under the sand dunes of the Bay of Skail, a great storm in 1850 uncovered this Stone Age village, which has been excavated.

The villagers dug holes into the sandy soil so that their homes were half underground, affording some

protection against the winds. Interconnecting passages between the huts were lined with sandstone slabs. Wandering around the site and looking down into these homes is a poignant experience. The layout of the rooms resembles any small peasant dwelling – except everything here, including the furniture, is made of stone. The dresser is a couple of flagstone shelves resting on stone 'legs', the bed is made of three slabs of stone set against the wall to form a 'box', and there is a central hearth.

There are few trees on Orkney, which is why the people of Skara Brae had to use alternative materials. Whale jawbones were probably used as rafters to support the roof, tools were made of bone and stone, and pottery was richly decorated. These ancient people were farmers who bred cows and sheep and grew grains. Looking into their homes makes their lives seem vivid and close. An excellent reconstruction of a stone house complete with a roof is well worth a visit.

✚ 25S ✉ 13km (8 miles) north of Stromness, Orkney
🕓 Apr–Sep Mon–Sun 9:30–5:30; Oct–Mar Mon–Sun 9–4:30
🖐 Moderate 🍴 Café (£)
ℹ Visitor centre
☎ 01856 841815

9 The Tenement House, Glasgow

www.nts.org.uk

Most of the population of industrial Scotland in the 19th and early 20th centuries lived in four- or five-storey tenement buildings similar to this one.

Miss Agnes Toward moved into this three-roomed flat with her mother in 1911 and lived there until her death in 1965. Houses in tenements ranged from the single end, which would nowadays be called a studio flat, to apartments such as this one, with several bedrooms and even a bathroom. Most apartments had no inside toilet but several families would share one toilet off the stairs. Better classes of tenement building were distinguished by the 'wally close', with ornate patterned ceramic tiles on the walls of the entry.

The kitchen of a tenement, with the cooking range for warmth, was the hub of family life. Miss Toward's kitchen utensils lie on the deal (fir or pine) table, her jars of home-made jam are still sealed above, the washboard is in the deep ceramic sink and the washing hangs to dry on the pulley. The bed, built into the recess in the kitchen, consists of a lumpy mattress on boards and snow-white bed linen, and there is a another bed tucked away below to accommodate the large families which were the norm.

When Miss Toward died it was discovered that she had never thrown anything away. She had kept bus tickets, letters booking her holidays, even newspapers, which were piled high on chairs and tables. It was a significant hoard of ephemera, portraying a way of life that was passing, a tiny fragment of history caught in amber, and nostalgia for those who can remember it.

✚ *Glasgow 3b* ✉ 145 Buccleuch Street, Garnethill, Glasgow ☎ 0844 493 2197 ⏰ Mar–Oct daily 1–5 (last entry 4:30) ✋ Moderate 🚌 From Buchanan Street Bus Station 🚊 Charing Cross

10 Traquair House

www.traquair.co.uk

Dating from the early 12th century, Traquair claims to be the oldest continually inhabited house in Scotland.

The house was originally built as a hunting lodge for the Scottish kings and queens. Because of its strategic position on the banks of the River Tweed, it was fortified against border raids. James III gave it to his court musician, who sold it to the Earl of Buchan for £3 15s. Buchan's son James Stuart became the first laird, and from then on it developed as a family home. The main section was completed around 1600 and another two wings were added a century later. The famous Bear Gates were erected in 1737 at a cost of £12 15s for the pillars, £10 4s for the carving of the stone bears and four gallons of ale for the workmen. The gates opened into a long tree-lined avenue which Prince Charles Edward Stuart trod one late autumn day in

1745 as he set off on his ill-fated venture to try to reclaim the throne for the House of Stuart. The Earl swore that they would never be opened again until a Stuart returned to the throne of Scotland. To this day they remain sealed.

The woodlands and gardens around Traquair are usually buzzing with activity – there are various craft

workshops and a brewery. The beer is brewed in the old brew-house and fermented in 200-year-old oak casks. The maze next to the house is a delight for children, while the house itself is a labyrinth, with lots of quirky little steps and corridors and secret passages. Above all, it still has the feel of a family home.

✚ 20K ✉ 2km (1.5 miles) south of Innerleithen ☎ 01896 830323 🕐 Jun–Aug daily 10:30–5; Apr, May, Sep daily 12–5; Oct daily 11–4; Nov weekends 11–3 (guided tours). Last admission 30 minutes before closing 💷 Moderate 🍴 Tea room (£) 🚌 62 from Edinburgh and Peebles to Innerleithen

Best things to do

Great places to have lunch

Café Hula (£–££)

Great selection of made-to-order sandwiches and more substantial dishes, many with an Iberian-Mediterranean twist.

✉ 321 Hope Street, Glasgow ☎ 0141 353 1660

The Ceilidh Place (££)

Fresh bread, hearty soups, a vegetarian option and home baking.

✉ West Argyll Street, Ullapool ☎ 01854 612103

Henderson's (£)

Well-known vegetarian restaurant serving tasty salads, hot dishes and desserts. Convivial atmosphere with occasional live music.

✉ 94 Hanover Street, Edinburgh ☎ 0131 225 2131

Hullabaloo Restaurant (££)

Innovative food with a great vegetarian selection. Reserve ahead.
✉ Robert Burns Centre, Mill Road, Dumfries ☎ 01387 259679

The Lemon Tree (£)

BBC Scotland broadcasts live shows from here. Good soups, vegetarian options and substantial fare.
✉ 5 West North Street, Aberdeen ☎ 01224 641122

Monty's (£–££)

Sophisticated dining in the evening, simple high-quality dishes at lunch time.
✉ 5 Mounthooly Street, Lerwick ☎ 01595 696555

78 St Vincent Street (£–££)

Imaginative, high-quality food. Fresh Scottish ingredients with continental flair.
✉ 78 St Vincent Street, Glasgow ☎ 0141 248 7878

Street Lights Coffee House and Bistro (£–££)

In this foodie's town on the Solway sightseeing trail, Street Lights knows how to make great coffee.
✉ 187 King Street, Castle Douglas ☎ 01556 504222

The Sunflower (££)

A charming restaurant down a Peebles sidestreet, serving simple, wholesome and tasty food. One of the best places to eat in this quaint Borders town.
✉ 4 Bridgegate, Peebles ☎ 01721 722420

Valvona and Crolla (££)

A wonderful Italian delicatessen (fresh pesto, pasta, cheeses, olives, wine), with a stylish café in the back.
✉ 19 Elm Row, Edinburgh ☎ 0131 556 6066

Best golf courses

Carnoustie: Championship-standard course north of Dundee.
☎ 01241 802270; www.carnoustiegolflinks.co.uk ✋ Round £115

Gullane: There are three courses at Gullane golf club, the longest being the number 1 course.
☎ 01620 842255 www.gullanegolfclub.com ✋ Round £27–£90

Royal Troon: A demanding par-71 links course on the west coast.
☎ 01292 311555; www.royaltroon.com ✋ Day ticket £60–£220

Haggs Castle: Good-value golfing on a par-72, just outside Glasgow.
☎ 0141 4271157; www.haggscastlegolfclub.com ✋ Round £45, day ticket £55

Muirfield: Muirfield's golfers wrote the sport's rules in the 18th century.
☎ 01620 842123; www.muirfield.org.uk ✋ Round £175

Old Prestwick: A par-71 links course just off the A79.
☎ 01292 671020; www.prestwickgc.co.uk ✋ Round £115, day ticket £170

Royal Dornoch: A beautiful heather- and gorse-clad course.
☎ 01862 810219; www.royaldornoch.com ✋ Round £92

St Andrews, Old Course: A par-72 links course known in the town regarded as the home of golf.
☎ 01334 466666; www.standrews.org.uk ✋ Round £130

Turnberry, Ailsa: Practise your swing at the Colin Montgomerie Academy before taking on this par-69.
☎ 01655 331000; www.westin.com/turnberry ✋ Round £180

Turnberry, Kintyre Arran: Sea views are a bonus of this par-72 course in Ayrshire.
☎ 01655 331000; www.westin.com/turnberry ✋ Round £120

Top activities

Climbing: the Highlands is the main venue for climbing, with Aviemore as the main centre; there are strenuous opportunities in the Southern Uplands.

Walking: well-marked long-distance trails (such as the West Highland Way, the Southern Upland Way) can be found through hills, mountains, moorlands and forests. There are also marked walks in country parks and estates.

Fishing: for salmon and trout fishing, get a day ticket from the appropriate private estate, angling club or local council. There is sea fishing at seaside resorts.

Golf: the national game. If you can't get on one of the championship courses try one of the municipal courses and private clubs that admit day visitors – Girvan, Ayrshire; Thornhill, Dumfriesshire; Strathaven, Lanarkshire; and the Gowf Club, Loudoun, near Galston, Ayrshire; (➤ 60–61).

Curling: Scotland's other national game is now an Olympic sport. Many towns and hotels have rinks and offer lessons. Dumfries Ice Bowl, the Magnum Leisure Centre, Irvine (➤ 126) and the Aberdeen Beach Leisure Centre are a few.

Birdwatching: there are many species to be spotted, from the ospreys at Grantown-on-Spey and puffins on Shetland to the Spitsbergen barnacle geese at Caerlaverock, Dumfries.

Bicycling: a great way to tour Scotland. There has been an increase in bicycle paths across the whole country. The 7Stanes mountain biking centres (➤ 100) across the borders and other centres have increased its popularity.

Watersports: sailing, canoeing, whitewater rafting, water-skiing, swimming, windsurfing – you name it, Scotland has it all. Venues include Raasay Outdoor Centre on an island near Skye (➤ 173), Strathclyde Park and Loch Ken Watersports in Dumfriesshire. Sea kayaking is an increasingly popular way of exploring the islands.

Whisky tasting: many of the world's oldest and most famous distilleries – including Bowmore and Highland Park – offer on-site tours and tastings of the end product, the 'water of life'.

Wildlife watching: highland safaris and wildlife-spotting hides at estates such as Rothiemurchus allow glimpses of elusive native animals including pine martens, Arctic hares and red deer.

a walk in Edinburgh

This walk takes in the Old Town of Edinburgh, including the historic Grassmarket, the Royal Mile and Greyfriars Church. The view from Calton Hill is spectacular.

Begin on Castle Esplanade. At the end, turn down the steps to the Grassmarket. Cross Johnstone Terrace and continue to the bottom. Turn left along the Grassmarket.

Investigate the attractive shops of Victoria Street to the left and return to the Grassmarket.

Cross over into Candlemaker Row and go up to the statue of Greyfriars Bobby.

To the right is Greyfriars Church, where the faithful little terrier, Greyfriars Bobby, kept vigil over his master's grave, and opposite is the Museum of Scotland (➤ 78–79).

Turn left along George IV Bridge, then right down the Royal Mile (➤ 81).

You will pass the cathedral, the Museum of Childhood (➤ 67) and John Knox's House. Holyroodhouse (➤ 79) and the Scottish Parliament are at the bottom (➤ 82).

Turn back up the Royal Mile to White Horse Close on the right. Go through it on to Calton Road. Turn left and take the steep steps on your right up to Regent Road. Cross and take the road leading up behind the Royal High School to Calton Hill.

On the way is a cairn dedicated to the achievement of a Scottish Parliament. On Calton Hill (➤ 77), pass the National Monument and Nelson's Monument.

Take the steps back to Regent Road. Turn right, cross the road and head towards Princes Street. After the Mound, enter Princes Street Gardens past the Floral Clock. Exit by the gate towards the castle and Ramsay Garden. Head up through Ramsay Garden and return.

Distance 6km (4 miles)
Time 2–6 hours
Start/end point Castle Esplanade ✚ *Edinburgh 2b*
Lunch Clarinda's Tea Room (£) ✉ 69 Canongate ☎ 0131 557 1888

Places to take the children

Ailsa Craig

This granite island is 13km (8 miles) off the Ayrshire coast and accessible by boat from Girvan. The source of all the world's curling stones and a bird sanctuary, it is hugely popular.

✉ Mark McCrindle at Girvan Harbour, 7 Harbour Street, Girvan ☎ 01465 713219

Codona's Amusement Park

Scotland's largest amusement park, with lots of major rides, kiddie rides, playground, video games and a roller coaster.

✉ Beach Boulevard, Aberdeen ☎ 01224 595910; www.codonas.com

Deep Sea World

Twenty minutes' drive, or a short train journey away from the city, brings you to this fascinating attraction dramatically situated beneath the Forth Rail Bridge. Over 2,000 fish, Europe's largest collection of tiger sharks and the world's longest walk-through underwater tunnel.

✉ Battery Quarry, North Queensferry ☎ 01383 411880; www.deepseaworld.co.uk

Dynamic Earth

This geological centre tells the story of our planet using special effects and the lastest in interactive technology. Witness meteor showers, see volcanoes erupting and visit tropical rainforests. There are computer programs for younger children.

✉ Holyrood Road, Edinburgh ☎ 0131 550 7800; www.dynamicearth.co.uk

Edinburgh Zoo

In hillside parkland, Edinburgh Zoo is world-renowned for its conservation work. The world's largest penguin enclosure has a 'Penguin Parade' at 2:15pm.

✉ Corstorphine Road, Murrayfield, Edinburgh ☎ 0131 334 9171;
www.edinburghzoo.org.uk

Glasgow Science Centre

Including an IMAX theatre, aerofoil-shaped viewing tower, the Science Mall and over 500 interactive exhibits.

✉ 50 Pacific Quay, Glasgow ☎ 0871 540 1000;
www.glasgowsciencecentre.org

Highland Wildlife Park

Drive-through reserve featuring birds and Scottish mammals of the past and present, including red deer, bison and the quintessentially Scottish Highland cattle.

✉ Kincraig, Kingussie, Aviemore ☎ 01540 651270;
www.highlandwildlifepark.org

Museum of Childhood

Superb free facility with toys from yesteryear; proof that there was life before computer games were invented.

✉ 42 High Street, Royal Mile, Edinburgh ☎ 0131 529 4142;
www.edinburgh.gov.uk

Puppet Theatre

A miniature Victorian theatre with seating for a hundred.

✉ Broughton Road on the B7016 east of Biggar ☎ 01899 220631

Serpentarium

More reptiles under one roof than you could ever imagine.

✉ The Old Mill, Harrapool, Broadford, Skye ☎ 01471 822209;
www.skyeserpentarium.org.uk

Stunning views

Edinburgh's Calton Hill
Hike up the hill for a panoramic view of Scotland's capital (➤ 77).

Foula
Watch the birds here (➤ 166) or at Ailsa Craig (➤ 66).

Glasgow
Look up when you walk around Glasgow to appreciate the city's architecture (➤ 102–106, 108–109).

Glen Coe
Drink in the view of the Three Sisters and the panorama looking down the Glen (➤ 44–45) .

Glens of Angus
Spot the red deer that roam the glens (➤ 134).

Isles of Jura and Mull
From the Isle of Kerrera in Oban Bay look towards the isles of Colonsay and Mull (➤ 142).

Loch Fyne
Enjoy the superb views of the loch from Crarae Garden (➤ 135).

Nevis Range
Take the gondola up Aonach Mor for views over the Great Glen, Nevis Range and towards the Irish Sea (➤ 161).

Skye
The black, jagged silhouette of the Cuillin mountains on Skye (➤ 172–174).

Tobermory Bay
The bay with its colourful houses from the Western Isles Hotel (➤ 149).

Celtic music and pubs

EDINBURGH
The Royal Oak
An ancient pub with regular sessions. The bar is one of the finest in Edinburgh, compact and intimate with a real fire. This is what pubs used to be like. Check the board outside for upcoming gigs.
✉ Infirmary Street, Edinburgh ☎ 0131 557 2976

Sandy Bell's Bar
This bar was once called the Forrest Hill Bar, but a previous manager was called Sandy Bell and the name stuck. The pub has a long history as a popular folk-music venue and comes into its own from about 9pm, when the bands begin to play.
✉ 25 Forrest Road, Edinburgh ☎ 0131 225 2751

The Tass
A fine Edinburgh folk pub, featuring sessions on Wednesday and Friday nights. Great pub food and real ales the rest of the time.
✉ Corner of High Street and St Mary's Street, Edinburgh ☎ 0131 556 6338

GLASGOW
The Scotia Bar
Once the haunt of Scottish comedian Billy Connolly, this pub hosts mostly blues and rock but there's also some folk and poetry.
✉ 112 Stockwell Street, Glasgow ☎ 0141 552 8681

Victoria Bar
Just round the corner from the Scotia (above), this is another favourite haunt of Glasgow musicians. Come on Friday night for folk sessions; Saturday and Sunday for live bands.
✉ 57 Bridgegate, Glasgow ☎ 014 552 6040

CENTRAL SCOTLAND
The Stables Inn
Named Music Pub of the Year 2009, the Stables is Scotland's

premier music
pub venue for
rock and folk
music gigs.
Great food,
rooms and
fantastic
atmosphere.

✉ Lathones, by Largoward, St Andrews ☎ 01334 840490;
www.mundellmusic.com

The Taybank

Home of the Acoustic Music Gallery, you can hear some of the
best Celtic music in Scotland but also learn to play it: guitar and
fiddle classes can be taken here.

✉ On the A984 road from Dunkeld to Coupar Angus ☎ 01350 727340;
www.thetaybank.com

THE NORTH
The Ceilidh Place

This versatile venue – there is a hotel, restaurant and book shop
too – offers line-ups of top-notch celtic musicians and bands.

✉ West Argyll Street, Ullapool ☎ 01854 612103; www.theceilidhplace.com

Hootananny

With three bars, ceilidh on Saturdays and live music from Sunday
to Wednesday, this is the top music venue in Scotland's north.

✉ 67 Church Street, Inverness ☎ 01463 233 651; www.hootananny.com

The Seaforth

A smart pub overlooking the harbour, and hosting eclectic live
music from Scottish indie bands to Celtic sounds and DJ nights.

✉ Quay Street, Ullapool ☎ 01854 612122; www.theseaforth.com

Exploring

Scotland occupies the upper third of Britain and some Scots would argue that the best has risen to the top. Certainly, it is geographically blessed: Britain's highest mountains, largest national park and deepest lakes are in Scotland. But it is also historically and culturally rich. Few nationalities have as distinctive an identity as the Scots and their world-famous exports whisky, golf and tartan – although haggis seems not to have caught on. Politically and historically, Edinburgh, the home of the Scottish Parliament, dominates Scottish life. But its rival to the west, Glasgow, has as much to offer culture vultures, with its unique architectural heritage. To appreciate the best of Scotland you should get off the beaten track: seek out remote seaside towns on the west coast where some of the most beautiful beaches in Europe lie, venture into the heather-clad Highlands or take a ferry to Scotland's enchanting islands.

Edinburgh and the Borders

Built on a series of volcanic rocks, Edinburgh, Scotland's capital, is undoubtedly among Europe's most beautiful cities. It offers a rich mix of architecture, first-rate museums and galleries, green spaces and shopping, and eating and entertainment.

Throughout the centuries, Edinburgh and its iconic castle was often the goal of marauding English armies, who marched through the borderlands to the south, besieging towns and castles and reiving (stealing) cattle. Despite this, the richness of the land brought prosperity, and enabled merchants to establish thriving market towns such as Haddington, Jedburgh, Kelso and Melrose, while the aristocracy left their mark with their defensive castles and grand mansions. Today, this legacy adds an extra dimension to exploring the Borders, where sightseeing goes hand in hand with superb opportunities for enjoying the countryside with its rolling hills and splendid rivers.

EDINBURGH

Incomparable Edinburgh combines its role as a capital city with inspirational architecture and a life-style for its citizens that's rated among the best in the world. The contrast between the narrow closes and winding streets of the Old Town and the spacious and classical streets of the New are the key to its allure, while its compact size and the friendliness of its people make it one of the most visitor-friendly cities imaginable.

Arthur's Seat

The plug of an ancient volcano forms Arthur's Seat, the highest of Edinburgh's seven hills and the focal point of the (265ha) 650-acre Holyrood Park. You can drive up to Dunsapie Loch and then walk up grassy slopes to the summit, which offers glorious and sweeping views of the city, the coast and the distant hills.

✚ *Off Edinburgh 6d*

Britannia

The former royal yacht came to Leith in 1998 and attracts visitor hordes to its excellent visitor centre, but the main enticement is the yacht itself. You can see the Queen's private quarters, the state reception rooms and the surprisingly cramped crew's accommodation.

www.royalyachtbritannia.co.uk

✚ *Edinburgh 4a (off map)* ✉ Ocean Terminal, Leith ☎ 0131 555 5566
🕐 Apr–Jun, Sep–Oct daily 10–4; Jul 9:30–4; Aug 9:30–4:30; Jan–Mar, Nov–Dec 10–3:30 🍴 Expensive 🍽 Excellent café (£) ❓ Reserve in advance, particularly in Aug

Calton Hill

Looming over the east end of Princes Street, Calton Hill offers great city-centre views and a wider panorama towards Fife. Its eccentric buildings include the City Observatory, the telescopic tower of the Nelson Monument, and the unfinished National Monument.

✚ *Edinburgh 4a*

Edinburgh Castle

Best places to see, ➤ 42–43.

Grassmarket

Dating from 1477, Edinburgh's original market is an attractive elongated space crammed with bars and restaurants, while the surrounding steeply climbing streets are home to some eclectic shops.

✚ *Edinburgh 2d–3c*

National Gallery Complex

Two splendid neoclassical buildings, designed by William Playfair in 1848, house Scotland's National Gallery and Royal Academy. The picture collection is superb, a glorious romp through the entire development of European painting, from the Byzantine-style Madonnas of the 14th century, through the Renaissance to the Impressionists. Don't miss the wonderfully quirky *Reverend Walker Skating on Duddingston Loch* by Raeburn, just one of the works by Scottish artists. The adjacent Royal Academy hosts temporary block-buster exhibitions.

www.nationalgalleries.org

🛨 *Edinburgh 2b* ✉ The Mound ☎ 0131 624 6200
🕐 Fri–Wed 10–5, Thu 10–7 ✋ Free 🍴 Good café (£)

National Museum of Scotland

Opened in 1998, with its airy, modern design incorporating traditional Scottish architectural elements, the National Museum tells Scotland's story through thousands of artefacts and exhibits, displayed thematically on seven floors. Pick and choose what takes your interest, but don't miss the Changing Nation section, devoted to modern Scots,

their lives and achievements. Kids will enjoy Connect, which has plenty of hands-on stuff.

www.nms.ac.uk

➕ *Edinburgh 3d* ✉ Chambers Street ☎ 0131 225 7534 🕐 Daily 10–5
✋ Free 🍴 Café (£)

New Town

The New Town is a superb 18th-century cityscape of gracious streets, crescents and gardens built on a grid pattern, an area for wandering for pleasure. It was built as an extension to the crowded and unhealthy tenements of the Royal Mile, and constructed to plans by James Craig, who won the competition commission in 1766. The street names honour the Hanoverian dynasty; even the layout reflects the design of the Union flag.

➕ *Edinburgh 2a*

Palace of Holyroodhouse

Holyrood is the Queen's official Scottish residence and the site has been home to Scottish monarchs since the 16th century. The present building dates from 1671 and guided audio tours take in the state apartments, while the lovely grounds contain the ruins of Holyrood Abbey, founded in 1128 and the scene of Scottish coronations and royal burials.

www.royal.gov.uk

➕ *Edinburgh 6b* ✉ Royal Mile ☎ 0131 556 5100 🕐 Apr–Oct daily 9:30–6; Nov–Mar 9:30–4:30 (closed 10 Apr, 25–26 Dec and during royal visits). Last admission 1 hour before closing ✋ Expensive
🍴 Good café/restaurant (£)

The People's Story

This fascinating social history museum is housed in the old Canongate Tolbooth, a former tax collecting house, court and prison. It tells the story of Edinburgh's ordinary citizens at work, home and play, from the late 18th century to the present day.
www.cac.org.uk

✚ *Edinburgh 5b* ✉ Canongate Tolbooth, Royal Mile ☎ 0131 529 4057
🕐 Mon–Sat 10–5 (Sun 12–5 during Aug only) ✋ Free

Princes Street

Princes Street is a superb, arrow-straight, Georgian-planned thoroughfare, backed by the grid of the New Town and fronted by Princes Street Gardens and the looming bulk of Edinburg Castle. Sadly, its original buildings are long gone, though nothing detracts

from the splendour of the Scott Monument, built in 1864 to honour Scotland's favourite novelist, or the verdant beauty of the gardens, laid out on the site of the old Nor' Loch and bridging the gap between the Old and New Towns.

✚ *Edinburgh 1b–3b*

Royal Botanic Garden

This noted botanical garden was founded around 200 years ago. The flower and shrub displays are at their best from spring to late autumn, and the 10 different glasshouses cover climates and their flora from all over the world.
www.rbge.org.uk

✚ *Edinburgh 4a (off map)* ✉ 20A Inverleith Row ☎ 0131 552 7171
🕐 Apr–Sep daily 10–7; Mar and Oct daily 10–6; Nov–Feb daily 10–4. Glasshouses Mar–Oct 10–5, Nov–Feb 10–3:30 ✋ Free, glasshouses moderate 🍴 Good café and restaurant

Royal Mile

Running from the Castle a mile downhill to Holyrood, the Royal Mile and its adjoining closes and vennels (alleyways) is packed with interest and history. Along its length you'll find myriad souvenir and tartan shops, whisky centres, bars and restaurants. Stroll down and take in the main sights, which include Gladstone's Land, a 16th-century merchant's house, St Giles, Edinburgh's main Presbyterian kirk (church), Parliament House, now used by lawyers, and John Knox's house. Museums include the Museum of Childhood, the Museum of Edinburgh and The People's Story (➤ 80); other attractions are Mary King's Close, a warren of underground medieval streets, and Our Dynamic Earth, a kid-friendly state-of-the-art geological centre.

 Edinburgh 3c–6b

Scottish National Gallery of Modern Art

This modern art collection covers everything from Matisse and Picasso to Jackson Pollock and Henry Moore, and occupies a gracious neoclassical building surrounded by a park dotted with sculpture.

www.nationalgalleries.org

➕ *Edinburgh 1c (off map)* ✉ Belford Road ☎ 0131 624 6200 🕓 Daily 10–5 ✋ Free 🍴 Excellent café/restaurant

The Scottish Parliament

Scotland achieved its first modern parliament in 1999, housed in Catalan architect Enric Miralles' complex and controversial building at Holyrood. A fusion of different materials, architectural elements and ideas, it's a remarkable structure, which incorporates Queensberry House, built in 1681. You can listen to debates, wander around, or take a guided tour.

www.scottish.parliament.uk

➕ *Edinburgh 6b* ✉ Royal Mile ☎ 0131 348 5200 🕓 Tue–Thu 9–6:30 (business days); Mon and Fri and all weekdays during recess Apr–Sep 10–5:30; Oct–Mar 10–4; Sat 11–5:30 all year ✋ Free; guided tours moderate 🍴 Café (£)

The Borders

ABBOTSFORD HOUSE

Sir Walter Scott (1771–1832) designed Abbotsford and lived there until his death. The Scots Baronial design, with medieval towers and turrets, reflects his romantic side. The library, housing Scott's rare books, is light and airy and also displays his accumulation of bizarre Scottish memorabilia, from Bonnie Prince Charlie's hair to the crucifix carried by Mary, Queen of Scots, when she was beheaded.

www.scottsabbotsford.co.uk

🕇 20K 🖂 3km (2 miles) west of Melrose ☎ 01896 752916 🕐 Jun–Sep daily 9:30–5; mid-Mar to May and Oct Mon–Sat 9:30–5, Sun 10–4
💷 Moderate 🍴 Tea room (£)

HADDINGTON

The historic town of Haddington, a mixture of broad tree-lined streets and medieval street plan, is an architectural delight. The High Street, with its lanes, narrow alleys and quaint shops, is fronted by the elegant Town House designed by William Adam. Nearby is the classical frontage of Carlyle House. The childhood home of Jane Welsh Carlyle, wife of Thomas Carlyle, the Sage of Chelsea, is tucked away behind it. Around the corner lies Haddington House, the oldest house in town, complete with re-created 17th-century garden. Further on, the tranquil riverside walk leads to St Mary's Collegiate Church, steeped in historical significance. The marks of the bombardment by the English during the 'Rough Wooing' are still visible. John Knox, the great Protestant reformer, preached here; the Lauderdale Aisle is an exquisite Episcopalian chapel; and two of the lovely stained-glass windows are by Sir Edward Burne-Jones.

Just beyond Haddington is **Lennoxlove**, set in 240ha (593 acres) of verdant woodlands. It appears to have grown in a mixture of styles around a medieval tower and has a collection of furniture, paintings and mementoes of Mary, Queen of Scots, including her death mask. Experienced guides relate the history of the house.

✛ 20J

Lennoxlove

✉ 3km (2 miles) south of Haddington ☎ 01620 823720; www.lennoxlove.org
🕙 Apr–Oct Wed, Thu and Sun 1:30–4, half hourly tours 👋 Moderate

JEDBURGH

This lovely little town with its old wynds (alleys) and houses was established as a Royal Burgh in the 12th century. The immense, graceful ruin of Jedburgh Abbey, founded in 1138, gives the most complete impression of all the Border abbeys' great monastic

institutions. It has a haunting abandoned feel to it, as if its medieval inhabitants might return next week to repair the roof.

The mellow 16th-century tower house, known as Mary Queen of Scots' House, is worth a visit, too. It wasn't actually her house but she did stay here.

www.historic-scotland.gov.uk

✛ 21K ✉ 16km (10 miles) southwest of Kelso ☎ 01835 863925 🕙 Apr–Sep daily 9:30–5:30; Oct–Mar Mon–Sat 9:30–4:30 👋 Inexpensive 🍴 Cafés and restaurants (£) nearby in town

❓ Opening times also apply to Dryburgh and Melrose abbeys

KELSO

The small market town of Kelso has an enormous cobbled square with a cluster of Georgian houses around it and a maze of cobbled streets leading off. Kelso Abbey suffered badly during the 'Rough Wooing' when Henry VIII tried to control the infant Mary, Queen of Scots, and not much remains. Floors Castle, a mile along the Cobby Riverside walk, is an early 18th-century mansion designed by William Adam and still home to the Duke of Roxburgh.

Mellerstain House, a few miles away, is possibly the finest Georgian mansion in Scotland, retaining the original tones in its interior paintwork. Allow half a day to take in the superb collection of paintings, period furniture and terraced gardens.

➕ 21K

Mellerstain House

✉ Gordon ☎ 01573 410225; www.mellerstain.com 🕐 May, Jun, Sep Wed, Sun; Jul, Aug Sun, Mon, Wed, Thu 12:30–5; Oct Sun only 12:30–5
💵 Moderate 🍴 Restaurant (££)

MELROSE

Nestling in the Eildon Hills, Melrose is yet another picturesque old abbey town. The heart of Robert the Bruce, who rebuilt the abbey, is buried somewhere within the church. Nearby is a Roman three-hill fort, at Newstead, and the **Trimontium Exhibition** in Market Square tells the story of the Roman frontier post and its people.

✚ 21K

Trimontium Exhibition

✉ The Ormiston, Market Square ☎ 01896 822651; www.trimontium.org
🕑 Apr–Oct daily 10:30–4:30 💷 Inexpensive

ROBERT SMAIL'S PRINTING WORKS, INNERLEITHEN

Robert Smail's High Street printing shop (1840) is perfectly preserved with lots of working exhibits, some of them hands-on.
www.nts.org.uk

✚ 20K ✉ 7–9 High Street, Innerleithen ☎ 0844 493 2259 🕑 Apr–Oct, Mon, Thu–Sat 12–5, Sun 1–5 💷 Moderate

a drive in Edinburgh and the Borders

From Princes Street head east along Waterloo Place and Regent Road, then turn right into London Road (A1). Follow it until you see signs for Haddington (▶ 84–85). Turn right and when your visit is completed, return to the A1 and follow the signs for Berwick-upon-Tweed. After 32km (20 miles), turn left on to the A1107 for Eyemouth, then at Coldingham take a left on to the B6438 to St Abbs (▶ 90). Return via the B6438 to the A1, then turn left and continue until the turning for Duns on the A6105.

Chirnside, which you will pass, was the home of local farmer Jim Clark (1936–68) who was the world motor racing champion twice in the 1960s. Duns, the next town, has a museum dedicated to his life (44 Newtown Street).

From Duns follow the A6105 for 29km (18 miles) to its intersection with the A68, turn left and then in a short distance turn right on to the A6091 until you reach Galashiels, where you need to turn left on to the A72.

At Innerleithen you will find Robert Smail's Printing Works (► 87), and nearby is Traquair House (► 54–55).

Continue on the A72 until it joins the A702 just beyond Skirling. Turn left for Biggar.

In Biggar is the last gas works in Scotland, preserved as a museum; Gladstone Court, an indoor museum of old shops; and the Biggar Puppet Theatre (► 67).

Leave Biggar (A702) heading back the way you came, toward Edinburgh. After 29km (18 miles), turn right on to the A766 for Penicuik.

Here you will find the Edinburgh Crystal Visitor Centre.

Take the A701 from Penicuik, follow the signs for Roslin village and Rosslyn Chapel (► 48–49), then return to the A701 and follow the signs back to Edinburgh.

Distance 265km (165 miles)
Time 6–8 hours, depending on stops
Start point Princes Street 🚉 *Edinburgh 1b–3b*
End point Edinburgh 🚉 20J
Lunch Tontine Hotel (► 93, £) ✉ High Street, Peebles (after Innerleithen)

ROSSLYN CHAPEL

Best places to see, ➤ 48–49.

ST ABBS

St Abbs is a working fishing village. You can take a boat trip to get a closer look at the guillemots, kittiwakes, fulmars and razorbills which sweep and squeal and nest around the surrounding rocks and cliffs. Diving, to view the spectacular underwater scenery and sea life in these clear waters, is also possible. The nature reserve, near the village, offers rock-pool rambles and armchair dives, or you can follow the footpath to the lighthouse to appreciate the wonderful coastline and bird life.

✚ 22J ⅋ Café (£) near waterfront

TRAQUAIR HOUSE

Best places to see, ➤ 54–55.

HOTELS

EDINBURGH

The Abbey Hotel (£–££)

Small private hotel on a quiet Georgian terrace in good location; it offers large rooms, friendly staff and excellent value for money.

✉ 9 Royal Terrace ☎ 0131 557 0022; www.townhousehotels.co.uk

Apex International (££–£££)

Situated in the heart of the Old Town with superb views of the castle and close to lots of nightlife.

✉ 31–35 Grassmarket ☎ 0131 300 3456; www.apexhotels.co.uk

Balmoral (£££)

Forte's flagship hotel is an imposing Edwardian building overlooking the east end of Princes Street.

✉ 1 Princes Street ☎ 0131 556 2414; www.thebalmoralhotel.com

Bonham (££–£££)

A boutique hotel on the edge of Dean Village and minutes from Princes Street. Each bedroom is individually designed.

✉ 35 Drumsheugh Gardens ☎ 0131 226 6050; www.thebonham.com

Edinburgh Central SYHA Hostel (£)

This five-star hostel, near Princes Street, has modern rooms from singles to family size, a café, bistro and bar, WiFi and friendly staff.

✉ 9 Haddington Place ☎ 0131 524 2090; www.syha.org.uk

Dene Guest House (£)

Down the hill on the edge of the New Town, this welcoming guest house has 19 airy, clean rooms, all with bathrooms.

✉ 7 Eyre Place ☎ 0131 556 2700; www.deneguesthouse.com

Dunstane City Hotel (££)

There's boutique style and luxury at affordable prices at this recently refurbished town house hotel in the Haymarket.

✉ 5 Hampton Terrace, Haymarket ☎ 0131 337 6169; www.dunstane-hotel-edinburgh.co.uk

Ibis (£)

In a trendy square just off the Royal Mile with practical modern rooms, self-service breakfast and near several good restaurants.

✉ 6 Hunter Square ☎ 0131 240 7000; www.ibishotel.com

Parliament House Hotel (££)

Just off the east end of Princes Street, this tucked-away hotel has stylish, contemporary rooms, some with great views.

✉ 15 Calton Hill ☎ 0131 478 4000; www.parliamenthouse-hotel.co.uk

The Point (££–£££)

Stylish, soft minimalism is found at this über-trendy converted space below the ramparts of the castle.

✉ 34 Bread Street ☎ 0131 221 5555; www.point-hotel.co.uk

BIGGAR
Skirling House (££)

One of Scotland's best guesthouses has just five rooms so book ahead to enjoy a special experience deep in lovely countryside.

✉ Skirling House, Skirling, by Biggar ☎ 01899 860274; www.skirlinghouse.com

GULLANE
The Open Arms (££–£££)

A charming country inn, opposite the castle ruins and right on the village green, that is renowned for its comfort and charm.

✉ Dirleton ☎ 01620 850241; www.openarmshotel.com

JEDBURGH
Spread Eagle House (£)

A small but comfortable hotel in the heart of this historic town.

✉ 20 High Street ☎ 01835 862870; www.spreadeaglejedburgh.co.uk

Allerton House (£)

On the edge of town, this late-Georgian country house has great comfort and a quiet situation and is renowned for its breakfasts.

✉ Oxnam Road ☎ 01835 869633; www.allertonhouse.co.uk

KELSO
Cross Keys (££)
This Georgian reconstruction of an old coaching inn is a superb base for exploring the region.

✉ 36–37 The Square ☎ 01573 223303; www.cross-keys-hotel.co.uk

MELROSE
Burts (££)
This early 18th-century building is the place to experience the best of 'Scotland's Natural Larder', not to mention an interesting selection of malt whiskies.

✉ Market Square ☎ 01896 822285; www.burtshotel.co.uk

George and Abbotsford Hotel (££)
An 18th-century former coaching inn with a good selection of bar meals, situated in an exceedingly pretty Borders town near Sir Walter Scott's Abbotsford House (▶ 83).

✉ High Street ☎ 01896 822308; www.georgeandabbotsford.co.uk

PEEBLES
The Horse Shoe Inn (££)
This restaurant with rooms is the best place to stay if you're looking for a fine-dining experience. Rooms are large and comfortable but the food's the star, either in the main restaurant (optional tasting menu) or the bistro.

✉ Eddleston, by Peebles ☎ 01721 730225; www.horseshoeinn.co.uk

The Tontine (£)
A friendly, family-run hotel right in the town centre, recently refurbished in traditional style with good restaurant and bistro.

✉ High Street ☎ 01721 720892; www.tontinehotel.com

ST BOSWELLS
Dryburgh Abbey Hotel (££)
This Baronial mansion is situated on the banks of the Tweed across from Dryburgh Abbey, with its own swimming pool.

✉ Dryburgh village, off the B6356 ☎ 01835 822261; www.dryburgh.co.uk

RESTAURANTS

EDINBURGH

Atrium (£££)

Mediterranean meets Midlothian here. Try the venison in cherry sauce with cabbage and bacon, and seared scallops as a starter.

✉ Cambridge Street ☎ 0131 228 8882

Bell's Diner (£)

Up and running for over 30 years, Bell's Diner is Edinburgh's independent burger joint extraordinaire. Great meat, generous plates and friendly staff add up to a value for money and delicious eating experience.

✉ 7 St Stephen's Street, Stockbridge ☎ 0131 225 8116

The Deep Sea (£)

Not far down the Leith Walk, the scent of frying and vinegar wafts out from this renowned chippie, where you'll find excellent – and excellent value – fish and chips. Everything is freshly fried.

✉ Leith Walk (opposite Playhouse Theatre) ☎ No telephone

Dusit (££)

Head here for some superlative Thai cooking, using the freshest of seafood, also chicken and meat. Subtle spicing with plenty of kick makes eating here a real pleasure for a change of pace.

✉ 49 Thistle Street ☎ 0131 220 6846

Henderson's (£)

See page 58.

The Kitchin (£££)

This Michelin-starred restaurant has taken Edinburgh by storm with its relaxed ambiance, impeccably sourced ingredients and imaginative cooking – all served up with efficiency and charm.

✉ 78 Commercial Quay, Leith ☎ 0845 202 6179

Urban Angel (£–££)

A great little deli and café, specializing in organic, seasonal and ethically sourced dishes. Delicious salads and baking throughout the day and more substantial lunch and evening specialities.

✉ 121 Hanover Street ☎ 0131 225 6215

Valvona and Crolla (££)

See page 59.

The Witchery by the Castle and Secret Garden (£££)

An imposing 16th-century building at the gates of Edinburgh Castle houses these two atmospheric venues in one. The Witchery's sumptuous menu features the best in Scottish cuisine. The Secret Garden downstairs looks onto the terrace and offers the same quality food and fat winelist – the full appreciation of which may require you to book one of the opulent suites above.

✉ 352 Castle Hill, Royal Mile ☎ 0131 225 5613; www.thewitchery.com

BIGGAR
Restaurant 55 (£–££)

Right in the town centre, this relaxed place serves modern Scottish food, using local and seasonal produce, in modern surroundings.

✉ 55 High Street ☎ 01899 231555

GULLANE
La Potinière (££)

Situated just 30 minutes from Edinburgh, this very popular restaurant offers good food and a warm and relaxed atmosphere. Needs to be reserved well in advance.

✉ Main Street ☎ 01620 843214

KELSO
The Cobbles Inn (£)

This old coaching inn has been modernized to provide the setting for a gastro-pub serving an eclectic menu – expect everything from local steak, modern European and fusion Pacific Rim cuisine. Real ales and continental beers are on offer.

✉ 7 Beaumont Street ☎ 01573 223548

Roxburghe Hotel and Golf Course (££)

Very popular with the huntin', fishin' and shootin' set. The Duke's estate supplies the Tweed salmon and wild game featured on the menu. Non-guests need to reserve in advance.

✉ Heiton (5km/3 miles southwest of Kelso on the A698) ☎ 01573 450331; www.roxburghe.net

MELROSE
Burt's Hotel (££)

Burt's, famous for its beef obtained from quality-assured farms, is a member of the Scotch Beef Club. The modern menu also features dishes such as chicken and sausage haggis and a lasagne of salmon and halibut served with ratatouille.

✉ Market Square ☎ 01896 822285; www.burtshotel.co.uk

Marmion's (£–££)

Melrose's most popular and best bistro has been pleasing locals and visitors for years with its great selection of staple dishes – baked potatoes, salads and hot dishes at lunch and a wider, more exciting choice in the evenings.

✉ Buccleuch Street ☎ 01896 822245

PEEBLES
Cringletie House Hotel (£££)

Chef Jimmy Desrivieres uses organic, wild and regional produce in an imaginative way to produce such delights as courgette (zucchini) and rosemary soup with crème fraîche.

✉ 3km (2 miles) north on the A703 ☎ 01721 725750; www.cringletie.com

The Sunflower (££)

See page 59.

SWINTON
Wheatsheaf Hotel (££)

Small hotel on the village green with friendly and attentive service. The menu features wood pigeon, duck and corn-fed chicken.

✉ Main Street ☎ 01890 860257; www.wheatsheaf-swinton.co.uk

SHOPPING

TWEEDS, TARTANS AND WOOLLIES

Belinda Robertson

If it's designer cashmere you want, this is the place for you. Along with sweaters, scarves and gloves, you can buy the latest in designer cashmere knickers, popular with the likes of Madonna.

✉ 13a Dundas Street, Edinburgh ☎ 0131 557 8118; www.belindarobertson.com

Geoffrey (Tailor)

This is the best source of tartan in all of Edinburgh. Kilts, both for men and women, off-the-rack or made-to-measure. Ex-rental garments for sale and all the usual accessories at a good price.

✉ 57–61 High Street, Edinburgh ☎ 0131 557 0256; www.geoffreykilts.co.uk

Kinloch Anderson

Get your tartan trews, kilts and accessories here and learn about the history of tartan in this Leith shop, in business since 1868.

✉ Commercial Street/Dock Street, Leith, Edinburgh ☎ 0131 555 1390; www.kinlochanderson.com

Peter Scott

Established over a century ago, this local firm specializes in knitwear, including top-quality wool and cashmere.

✉ 11 Buccleuch Street, Hawick ☎ 01450 364815; www.peterscott.co.uk

Ragamuffin

Scottish knitwear with a twist. Jerseys, jackets and accessories made on Skye in funky designs and a rainbow of colours.

✉ 278 Canongate ☎ 0131 557 6007

ANTIQUES AND COLLECTABLES

Byzantium

Antiques-cum-flea market. An eclectic collection of shops in one building full of antiques, books, prints and more – great for browsing. There's a restaurant on the top floor.

✉ 9 Victoria Street, Edinburgh ☎ 0131 225 1768

Carson Clark

A seriously dangerous shop for those addicted to antique prints and maps. Wonderful, hand-painted reproductions.

✉ 181–183 Canongate, Edinburgh ☎ 0131 556 471

Dead Head Comics

Shop for early *Superman* comics, science fiction and adventure.

✉ 27 Candlemaker Row, Edinburgh ☎ 0131 226 2774

Georgian Antiques

You'll find Edinburgh's largest collection of antiques, ephemera and collectables in this huge converted warehouse down in Leith.

✉ 10 Pattison Street, Leith ☎ 0131 553 7286

BOOKS
Analogue

Unusual book shop that stocks design and contempoary culture books. Also good for magazines, posters and T-shirts.

✉ 102 West Bow, Edinburgh ☎ 0131 220 0601; www.analoguebooks.co.uk

Armchair Books

There are thousands of second-hand books here, with the emphasis on Victorian, illustrated and antiquarian books – come prepared to browse.

✉ 72–74 West Port ☎ 0131 229 5927

Old Town Bookshop

If you are interested in Scotland and its writers, this is the place for second-hand books. Other subjects include music, travel and art.

✉ 8 Victoria Street, Edinburgh ☎ 0131 225 9237; www.oldtownbookshop.com

WHISKY
Royal Mile Whiskies

If you can resist the mouth-watering window display you don't need to buy whisky. Opposite St Giles Cathedral.

✉ 379 High Street ☎ 0131 225 3383; www.royalmilewhiskies.com

William Cadenhead

This small shop has a great selection of whiskies.

✉ 172 Canongate, Edinburgh ☎ 0131 556 5864; www.wmcadenhead.com

FOOD AND DRINK

Charles MacSween & Son

MacSween haggis is available in shops and supermarkets all over Scotland, but visit the factory to buy the freshest product.

✉ Dryden Road, Bilston Glen, Loanhead (just off the A768), Edinburgh
☎ 0131 440 2555; www.macsween.co.uk

Ian Mellis

The traditional cheesemonger stocks the most amazing range of Scottish cheeses. You can sample before you buy. Great oatcakes.

✉ 30 Victoria Street, Edinburgh ☎ 0131 226 6215;
www.ijmellischeesemonger.com

Valvona and Crolla

This is where Scotland's Italian community comes to shop. Fresh produce is shipped in weekly from Italy. Also has a café (► 59).

✉ 19 Elm Row, Edinburgh ☎ 0131 556 6066; www.valvonacrolla.co.uk

ENTERTAINMENT

Bongo Club

A café by day, the Bongo Club morphs into a multimedia venue after 7pm, with theatre, art exhibitions and music.

✉ Moray House, 37 Holyrood Road, Edinburgh ☎ 0131 558 7604;
www.thebongoclub.co.uk

Bow Bar

If it's traditional Scottish you want from a pub, try this one with its choice of over 140 malt whiskies. Good atmosphere.

✉ 80 West Bow, Edinburgh ☎ 0131 226 7667

Edinburgh Festival Theatre

One of the city's top theatres with a greatly varied schedule.

✉ 13–29 Nicholson Street, Edinburgh ☎ 0131 529 6000; www.eft.co.uk

Espionage

Five-level late, late complex with lounges, bars and clubs; lively, young and frequent promos.

✉ 4 India Buildings, Victoria Street ☎ 0131 477 7007; www.espionage007.co.uk

The King's Theatre

Magnificently refurbished, with a changing popular agenda.

✉ 2 Leven Street, Tollcross, Edinburgh ☎ 0131 529 6000; www.eft.co.uk

The Royal Oak

See page 70.

Sandy Bell's Bar

See page 70.

The Tass

See page 70.

SPORT

Edinburgh International Climbing Arena

The world's largest indoor climbing arena, complete with bouldering room and fitness suite.

✉ South Platt Hill, Ratho, Newbridge, Edinburgh ☎ 0131 333 6333; www.eica-ratho.com

Midlothian Snow Sports Centre

This municipal facility, with its massive artificial, year-round slope, has equipment rental and lessons. Reserve in advance.

✉ Hillend, on the A702 Edinburgh to Biggar road ☎ 0131 445 4433

Tweed Valley 7Stanes

Scotland's second most-visited attraction is this mountain biking centre in Glentress forest. The centre has a good café, shop and guides. Trails are graded like ski runs. Rental bicycles are available.

✉ Two miles south of Peebles ☎ 01721 721736; www.7stanes.gov.uk; www.thehubintheforest.co.uk

Glasgow and the Southwest

Glasgow is a fine Victorian city, built on the fortunes of the British Empire. Industry provided the impetus that saw it emerge as a city poles apart from Edinburgh – brash, commercial and extrovert. Today, after mid-20th-century decline, Glasgow's re-emerged as a confident and prosperous city, renowned for its style and the incredible friendliness of its people.

In this area you will find the industrial heart of Scotland, the shipyards of the Clyde, fast-moving computer production, sleepy rural backwaters, the wildernesses of Galloway and miles of coastline. It is a microcosm of Scottish industry, history and literature. Two popular poets, penicillin, tarmacadam, the mackintosh, the bicycle and the pneumatic tyre, not to mention Robert the Bruce and William Wallace, all emerged from the southwest of Scotland.

GLASGOW

Since its portrayal in Alexander McArthur and Kingsley Long's 1935 novel *No Mean City* as a wild, gangster-dominated place, Glasgow has reinvented itself several times. The Garden Festival transformed the derelict dock areas along the Clyde, while its role as European City of Culture in 1990 and City of Architecture 1999 proclaimed the stylishness of Glasgow.

World-renowned architects such as Charles Rennie Mackintosh and Alexander 'Greek' Thomson produced what has become one of Europe's best preserved Victorian cities. Imaginative modern designs, including the Burrell Collection and the Armadillo (the Scottish Exhibition and Conference Centre, a modern venue on the banks of the Clyde), maintain the standard while 1960s and 1970s architectural blight gradually disappears.

Burrell Collection

Best places to see, ➤ 38–39.

Gallery of Modern Art

This popular and witty gallery has undermined even the worthy statue of Wellington which fronts it. The great man and his horse are constantly adorned with traffic cones for headgear. In the entrance, the irreverent tone is set by the brilliant, papier mâché caricature of the Queen as a Glasgow housewife, in dressing gown and slippers, with dangling cigarette. The collection of art by living artists is housed on four floors.

www.glasgowmuseums.com

🔢 *Glasgow 4c* ✉ Royal Exchange Square ☎ 0141 287 3050
🕐 Mon–Wed, Sat 10–5, Thu 10–8, Fri, Sun 11–5 💷 Free 🍴 Excellent café (£) on premises

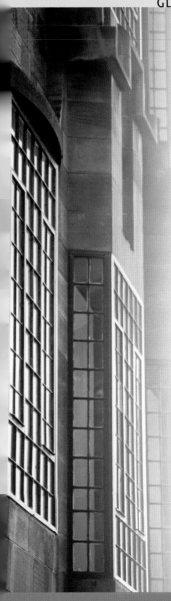

Glasgow School of Art

Charles Rennie Mackintosh won the competition to design the new school in 1896. It is the earliest example in the UK of a complete art nouveau building, including the interior furnishings and fittings. Students today still remove books from Mackintosh bookcases and sit on priceless Mackintosh chairs.

www.gsa.ac.uk

✚ *Glasgow 3b* ✉ 167 Renfrew Street ☎ 0141 353 4526 ⏰ Guided tours only Mon–Fri 11, 2, Sat 10:30, 11:30; extra tours Apr–Sep daily 11, 1:30, 2, 2:30 ✋ Moderate

🍴 Mackintosh's Willow Tea Room (£) is nearby at 217 Sauchiehall Street

103

Holmwood House

Restored by the National Trust for Scotland, Holmwood House, designed by Alexander 'Greek' Thomson, is one of Scotland's finest private villas. The paper magnate James Couper gave Thomson a free hand and he devised an astonishing asymmetrical design. One side has a flat classical frontage with pillars framing the dining room windows while the bay window on the other side is essentially a circular Greek temple, complete with free-standing pillars, fronting a timber and glass wall. None of the furniture remains but underneath the layers of paper, a remarkable amount of the original paint work has survived, including painted scenes of the Trojan Wars.

www.nts.org.uk

✚ *Glasgow 4d (off map)* ✉ 61 Netherlee Road, Cathcart ☎ 0844 493 2204 ⏰ Apr–Oct Thu–Mon 12–5 ♨ Moderate 🍴 Refreshments in Kitchen Court (£) 🚌 44 🚉 Glasgow Central (Neilston train to Cathcart station)

Kelvingrove Art Gallery and Museum

This elaborately turreted mansion, built of red Dumfriesshire sandstone stands on the banks of the River Kelvin. Its art collection includes works by Botticelli, the Pre-Raphaelites, the Impressionists and David Hockney, as well as many great Scottish artists, such as the Glasgow Boys (➤ 113). The museum has collections ranging from Egyptology and prehistory to ship-building and natural history and a Mini Museum for under 5s.

www.glasgowmuseums.com

✚ *Glasgow 2a* ✉ Argyle Street ☎ 0141 276 9599 🕐 Mon–Thu, Sat 10–5, Fri, Sun 11–5 🍽 Café and restaurant (£) 🚇 Kelvinhall

Museum of Transport

Displays cover the history of Scottish transportation, including the pioneer days of the Scottish motor industry. Cars include early Arrol Johnstones produced in Dumfries and the Hillman Imp, built at the long-closed Chrysler plant at Linwood. There is also a series of trams, the famous  'Shooglies', the earliest with gleaming brass and polished wood, as well as a 1938 street scene with a working cinema and a Victorian underground station.

www.glasgowmuseums.com

✚ *Glasgow 2a* ✉ 1 Bunhouse Road ☎ 0141 287 2664 🕐 Mon, Thu, Sat 10–5, Fri, Sun 11–5 ✋ Free 🍽 Café (£)

Scotland Street School Museum

Designed by Charles Rennie Mackintosh, this is an architectural gem, featuring two massive glass-fronted towers. Inside it re-creates the school experience of Scots children from Victorian times through to the 1950s. Classrooms have been reconstructed for several of the periods and, during school terms, visitors in the viewing galleries can watch local children and their teachers dress up in period costume and experience what it was like. Modern kids sometimes feel strange as their friendly teacher is transformed into the dragon of the Victorian classroom. At play time the youngsters take part in games from yesteryear. There are wooden spinning tops and girds and cleeks (hoops and sticks). The only problem for children is keeping the toys away from the grown-ups.

www.glasgowmuseums.com

✚ *Glasgow 3d* ✉ 225 Scotland Street ☎ 0141 287 0500 ⏰ Mon–Thu and Sat 10–5, Fri and Sun 11–5 ✋ Free 🍴 Café and vending machine area (£)

The Tall Ship at Glasgow Harbour

The River Clyde dominated world ship-building well into the 20th century. Many of the legendary liners, the *Queen Mary*, *Queen Elizabeth* and the *QE2*, were built here as well as other less famous ships. *The Glenlee* (1896) is one of the last of the Clyde-built sailing ships and one of only six still afloat. It was in the service of the Spanish navy until the 1970s. Acquired by the Clyde Maritime Trust, which has spent years restoring it, this steel-hulled cargo ship is one of Glasgow's newest attractions.

www.thetallship.com

✚ *Glasgow 1b* ✉ Yorkhill Quay, 100 Stobcross Road ☎ 0141 222 2536 ⏰ Mar–Oct daily 10–5; Nov–Feb daily 10–4 ✋ Moderate 🍴 Café (£)

The Tenement House, Glasgow

Best places to see, ➤ 52–53.

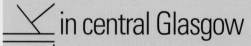

a walk in central Glasgow

This walk around central Glasgow takes in some of the city's most interesting architecture.

From the tourist office in George Square turn right then right on to Miller Street, left along Ingram Street and right on to Glassford Street.

The Tobacco Lairds House is on Miller Street. Glasgow's oldest secular building is the Trades Hall in Glassford Street, designed by Robert Adam in 1794.

Turn left on to Wilson Street, right at Candleriggs and left along the Trongate. Turn right on to Saltmarket and left on to Glasgow Green. Follow paths to the People's Palace and beyond that to Templeton Business Centre.

Modelled on the Palazzo Ducale in Venice, the multi-hued, richly patterned Templeton Business Centre was originally a Victorian carpet factory.

Return to the gates of Glasgow Green and go along Clyde Street. Turn right on to Jamaica Street, right on to Howard Street and left to St Enoch Square. Across Argyle Street head along Buchanan Street. Walk around Royal Exchange Square on the right. Continue on Buchanan Street then left along St Vincent Street.

In St Enoch Square the former underground station resembles a miniature château. St Vincent Street Church is the only surviving church of the Victorian architect Alexander 'Greek' Thomson.

Turn right up Pitt Street and right on to Renfrew Street, right at Dalhousie Street and left on Sauchiehall Street.

In Sauchiehall Street is another Thomson design, the former Grecian Chambers, and the Willow Tea Rooms, owned by Kate Cranston.

At Buchanan Street turn right, then left along West George Street to return to George Square.

Distance 5–6.5km (3–4 miles)
Time 4 hours
Start/end point George Square ✚ *Glasgow 4c*
Lunch 78 St Vincent Street (➤ 59)

The Southwest

ARRAN

Reached by Calmac ferry from Gourock, Arran is a delight. The main town of Brodick with its castle and gardens can be explored in a day trip, but it will take a few days to visit the standing stones on Machrie Moor, climb Goatfell or watch the sunset over Ailsa Craig from the south coast. Pottery, paintings, textiles, basketwork and glass, as well as cheese and whisky, are produced locally.

🚩 16K 🍴 Excellent cafés in Brodick (£) ⛴ Calmac Ferry from Gourock

BURNS NATIONAL HERITAGE PARK

Best places to see, ➤ 36–37.

CAERLAVEROCK CASTLE AND WILDFOWL AND WETLANDS TRUST RESERVE

Thirteenth-century **Caerlaverock Castle,** dramatically situated on the estuary of the River Nith, is the only triangular castle in Britain. Built of red sandstone, with a double-towered gatehouse, it was protected by a moat and huge ramparts. The castle was besieged, damaged and rebuilt by Scottish and English alike, and changed hands many times, particularly during the Wars of Independence (1296–1328). Inside there are the remains of a fine Renaissance mansion house built around 1620. It was finally left a ruin by the depredations of the Covenanters (Scots Protestants) a few years later. Further along the Solway is the **Wildfowl and Wetlands Trust Reserve** where acres of Merseland (mud flats and salt marshes) are conserved to protect the wildlife and to allow visitors to observe from hides. Caerlaverock is home to the most northerly colony of natterjack toads, and every summer the entire Spitsbergen colony of barnacle geese arrives. Activities for all age groups include everything from listening to the natterjack toads to watching badgers and seeing wild geese take flight.

Caerlaverock Castle

➕ 19L ✉ Near Bankend on B725 13km (8 miles) south of Dumfries ☎ 01387 770244; www.historic-scotland.gov.uk ⏰ Apr–Sep daily 9:30–6; Oct–Mar 9:30–4:30 🖐 Moderate 🍴 Café (£) 🚌 371 from Dumfries

Wildfowl and Wetlands Trust Reserve

☎ 01387 770200; www.wwt.org.uk ⏰ Daily 10–5 🖐 Moderate 🍴 Café (£)

CULZEAN CASTLE AND COUNTRY PARK

Perched on a cliff top over the Firth of Clyde, Culzean was constructed for the 10th Earl of Cassillis by the architect Robert Adam. After 20 years it was finally finished in 1792. Built in neo-Gothic style, with towers and turrets on the outside, the classical design of the interior is dominated by the majestic oval staircase. During his lifetime, the former US President Dwight D Eisenhower had the use of the top floor, and his life and work are commemorated in a permanent display. The castle is set in an extensive country park with gardens, seashore, wooded walks and a pond.

➕ 17K ✉ 19km (12 miles) southwest of Ayr on A719 near Maybole ☎ 01655 884455 ⏰ Castle and Walled Garden Apr–Oct 10:30–5. Visitor centre Apr–Oct 9–5:30; Nov–Mar Sat, Sun 11–4. Park daily 9:30–sunset 🖐 Expensive 🍴 Restaurant and coffee shop (£–££) 🚌 60 from Ayr

DUMFRIES

This quiet county town was home to two of Scotland's literary greats, Robert Burns and J M Barrie. Robert Burns, after an unsuccessful farming venture at nearby Ellisland, moved to Dumfries and worked as an excise man until his untimely death.

Robert Burns' house is now a museum and on display are the bed he died in and the desk where he penned the words of 'Auld Lang Syne'. In the Globe Inn, visitors can sit in the poet's chair but must recite a verse of his poetry or buy the assembled company a drink.

JM Barrie attended Dumfries Academy, and it was while playing pirates with his friends in a garden next to the school that Peter Pan was born. The garden was the inspiration for Never Never Land and Captain Hook was his maths teacher. In Dumfries Museum, the earliest example of Barrie's writing can be seen.

✚ 19L

Robert Burns House
✉ Burns Street ☎ 01387 255297 ⏰ Apr–Sep Mon–Sat 10–5, Sun 2–5; Oct–Mar Tue–Sat 10–1, 2–5 💷 Free

GALLOWAY FOREST PARK AND GLEN TROOL

The Galloway Forest Park centred around lovely Loch Trool and the Galloway Hills is an area of outstanding natural beauty. Hill-walking in this empty wilderness is rewarded by splendid views over lochs, hills and coast. Less strenuous is a stroll or bicycle through the myriad forest paths or a drive along the Queen's Way to the pretty village of New Galloway. The park's rangers host an extensive calendar of activities throughout the year, from wildlife-spotting walks to special events for children. There is also an excellent mountain bike park in the Kirroughtree area of the forest.

www.forestry.gov.uk/gallowayforestpark

✚ 18L ☎ 01671 402420 🍴 Cafés and tea rooms (£) at various villages and towns throughout the park

KIRKCUDBRIGHT

There is a magical quality to the light in this part of the world that seems to draw artists to the area. The illustrator Jessie M King and her husband, E A Taylor, lived at Green Gate Close on High Street, while Edward Hornel, one of the Glasgow Boys, a group of Scottish painters inspired by the Impressionists, lived nearby at **Broughton House.** Hornel's Georgian mansion, with its Japanese garden, is now a museum to his life and work. In the Old Tolbooth is an art centre featuring the work of local artists. Also worth a visit is the Stewartry Museum, with its archaeological, social history and natural history exhibts, and MacLellan's Castle, which dominates the square beside the picturesque working harbour.

✚ 18M

Broughton House

✉ High Street ☎ 01557 330437; www.nts.org.uk 🕐 Jul–Aug daily 12–5; Apr–Jun, Sep–Oct Thu–Mon 12–5. Garden only Feb, Mar Mon–Fri 11–4 🖐 Moderate

THIS MARKS THE TRADITIONAL SITE OF THE MARTYRDOM

THE MACHARS

South of Newton Stewart lies the peninsula of the Machars, a secluded agricultural area whose slow pace of life lends it a unique atmosphere. Quiet Wigtown, once a bustling place, is the main centre, and it's increasingly known for its numerous second-hand bookshops, earning Wigtown a role as Scotland's official 'book town'.

Further south is the sleepy town of Whithorn, where Chrisitianity first came to Scotland with St Ninian in AD397. Pilgrims flocked here from all over the Christian world until pilgrimage was banned during the Reformation. Much of medieval Whithorn remains, and at the **Whithorn Dig** the earlier settlements are being excavated.

✚ 18M

Whithorn Dig

✉ 45–47 George Street ☎ 01988 500508; www.whithorn.com ☀ Apr–Oct daily 10:30–5 ✋ Inexpensive

🍴 Central Café, 17 George Street (£)

NEW ABBEY

Nestling under Criffel, the village of New Abbey is dominated by the ruins of a Cistercian abbey. It was founded in 1273 by Devorgilla de Balliol, wife of the Scottish king

John Balliol, founder of Balliol College, Oxford and became known as **Sweetheart Abbey** because the hearts of Devorgilla and her husband are interred together here.

New Abbey Corn Mill is a water-driven mill, with working machinery. Near New Abbey is the museum of costume and dress at Shambellie House, and at Arbigland, near Kirkbean, is the cottage birthplace of John Paul Jones (1747–92), founder of the US Navy.

If the sky is clear a climb to Criffel's peak, 570m (1,870ft), will provide a view into Scotland, Ireland, England and the Isle of Man.

✚ 19L

Sweetheart Abbey

✉ New Abbey ☎ 01387 850397 ⏰ Apr–Sep daily 9:30–5:30; Oct–Mar Sat–Wed 9:30–4:30 ✋ Inexpensive 🍴 Tea room (£) 🚌 372 from Dumfries

New Abbey Corn Mill

✉ New Abbey ☎ 01387 850260; www.historic-scotland.gov.uk ⏰ Apr–Sep daily 9:30–5:30; Oct–Mar Sat–Wed 9:30–4:30 ✋ Moderate

NEW LANARK

Best places to see, ➤ 46–47.

SAMYE LING TIBETAN CENTRE

Probably the last thing you would expect to find in this remote and lonely corner of Dumfries and Galloway is a Buddhist monastery. Yet here it is in all its glory. Elaborate oriental buildings in bright red and gold sit high up in the Southern Uplands of Scotland with the tranquil sounds of wind chimes filling the air. Tibetan monks built Samye Ling, but it is home to a community of Buddhists. There are various courses in meditation available, including weekend workshops and retreats, and visitors are very welcome.

www.samyeling.org

✚ 20L ✉ Eskdalemuir ☎ 01387 373232 ⏰ Temple daily 6am–9pm ✋ Free 🍴 Café on site (£) 🚌 112 from Langholm

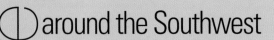 around the Southwest

This drive will take you through some of the finest scenery in Scotland – rugged mountains, rocky coastline, low-lying pastures and picturesque towns and villages.

From Dumfries follow the A710 via New Abbey, Kirkbean (➤ 115) and Colvend to Dalbeattie.

The John Paul Jones birthplace museum near Kirkbean is a tribute to the Scot who founded the American Navy. New Abbey is the site of Sweetheart Abbey and New Abbey Corn Mill (➤ 114–115).

From Dalbeattie take the A711 to Kirkcudbright, then the A762 to New Galloway.

Tiny Palnackie is the venue for the annual World Flounder Tramping Championships. Here competitors stand in the water, waiting until they feel a flounder moving under their feet, then reach down and scoop up the fish. At Dundrennan is another ruined abbey.

From New Galloway turn right on to the A712 to Balmaclellan, then the B7075 and right on to the A702 to Moniaive.

The clogmaker at Balmaclellan welcomes visitors to his workshop, while the picturesque village of Moniaive has a number of pleasant walks, as well as a good organic café, The Green Tea House.

Take the B729 just beyond Kirkland to Dunscore, then turn right on to a local road heading towards Newtonairds and follow the signs for Shawhead.

At Glenkiln Reservoir, a collection of sculptures by Henry Moore, Jacob Epstein and Auguste Rodin is displayed in the sweeping pastoral landscape. Moore's King and Queen sculpture on the hillside overlooking the reservoir has become the symbol of Glenkiln.

From Glenkiln continue along the side of the reservoir to Shawhead; follow the local road to the A75, turn left and return to Dumfries.

Distance 153km (95 miles)
Time 6–8 hours depending on stops
Start/end point Dumfries ✚ 19L
Lunch Craigdarroch Arms (➤ 123)

HOTELS

GLASGOW

Botanic Hotel (£)

Attractive Victorian terrace house in the West End close to the Botanic Garden, Kelvingrove and the transport museum.

✉ 1 Alfred Terrace ☎ 0141 337 7007; www.botanichotel.co.uk

City Inn Glasgow (££)

It may look a bit soulless outside, but the comfort, good value and superb riverside views fully make up for this. This is a good family choice.

✉ Finnieston Quay ☎ 0141 240 1002; www.cityinn.com/glasgow

Ewington Hotel (££)

A south-side town-house hotel, where kids go free. It's only six minutes by train to central Glasgow.

✉ Balmoral Terrace, 132 Queens Drive ☎ 0141 423 1152; www.mckeverhotels.co.uk

Kirklee Hotel (£)

A friendly three-star Edwardian-built guest house in a green, quiet suburb near the Botanic Garden – friendly owners and large comfortable rooms. The garden is lovely after a day's sightseeing.

✉ 11 Kensington Gate ☎ 0141 339 5555; www.kirkleehotel.co.uk

Millennium Hotel (£££)

Situated in the heart of the city close to all major attractions, excellent restaurants and the vibrant Glasgow nightlife. Bedrooms come in various sizes and there is a stylish brasserie.

✉ 50 George Square ☎ 0141 332 6711; www.millenniumhotels.com

One Devonshire Gardens (£££)

If you are looking for something elegant and sophisticated yet different, with legendary French and Scottish cuisine, stay here at this luxury boutique hotel.

✉ 1 Devonshire Gardens ☎ 0141 339 2001; www.onedevonshiregardens.com

The Townhouse (£–££)

Excellent accommodation in a graceful Georgian terraced house with lofty ceilings and big rooms. Very good value and prices include all the extras, such as WiFi, teamaking facilities etc.

✉ 21 Royal Crescent ☎ 0141 332 9009; www.townhousehotelglasgow.com

Victorian House (£)

Attractive house with 60 airy rooms ranging from singles to family suites. Good full Scottish breakfast.

✉ 212 Renfrew Street ☎ 0141 332 0129; www.thevictorian.co.uk

AUCHENCAIRN
Balcary Bay (£–££)

A 17th-century country house hotel on a picturesque bay. Scottish cuisine is based on local produce.

✉ Shore Road, near Castle Douglas ☎ 01556 640217;
www.balcary-bay-hotel.co.uk

AYR
Fairfield House (££)

There are fine views over the Firth of Clyde to Arran from this Victorian mansion which is close to central Ayr. Traditional country house hospitality is complemented by fine food.

✉ 12 Fairfield Road ☎ 01292 267461; www.fairfieldhotel.co.uk

BEATTOCK
Marchbankwood House (£)

There are lovely views from the grounds of this excellent guest house. Rooms are spacious and simply and comfortably furnished and there's a log fire in the lounge for chilly evenings.

✉ Beattock ☎ 01683 300118; www.marchbankwood.co.uk

CASTLE DOUGLAS
Douglas Arms (£)

This former coaching inn, recently refurbished, is well-loved for its friendly staff. Families are welcome.

✉ 206 King Street ☎ 01556 502231; www.douglasarmshotel.com

KIRKCUDBRIGHT
Fludha Guest House (££)
Beautifully set on a bend of the River Dee, is this very comfortable guesthouse. Excellent breakfasts feature smoked salmon and black pudding and dinner is also available.

✉ Tongland Road ☎ 01557 331443; www.fludha.com

Selkirk Arms (££)
Lord Peter Wimsey, Dorothy L Sayer's fictional detective, lodged in this fine 18th-century hotel in the novel *The Five Red Herrings* and Robert Burns wrote his famous *Selkirk Grace* here.

✉ High Street ☎ 01557 330402; www.bestwestern.com

MOFFAT
The Star (£)
This wonderful little hotel appears in the *Guinness Book of Records* as the narrowest hotel in the world.

✉ 44 High Street ☎ 01683 220156; www.famousstarhotel.com

NEWTON STEWART
Kirroughtree House (££)
A 17th-century country mansion, the Kirroughtree is a superb time capsule of a more gracious age.

✉ Newton Stewart ☎ 01671 402141; www.kirroughtreehouse.com

PORTPATRICK
Fernhill (££)
Dramatically perched on a hill overlooking the harbour and village of Portpatrick, Fernhill is at the start of the Southern Upland Way.

✉ Heugh Road ☎ 01776 810220; www.fernhillhotel.co.uk

STRANRAER
Corsewall Lighthouse Hotel (£££)
Wonderful coastal views from a converted lighthouse add to the charms of this hotel; some rooms are on the small side, but the purpose-built additions are roomier. Good restaurant.

✉ Corsewall ☎ 01776 853220; www.lighthousehotel.co.uk

THORNHILL
Trigony House (££)
Former Edwardian hunting lodge set in secluded gardens and famed locally for its excellent cuisine.

✉ Closeburn (1.5km/1 mile south off the A76) ☎ 01848 331211; www.trigonyhotel.co.uk

TURNBERRY
Westin Turnberry Resort (£££)
This world-famous hotel has one of the grandest views in Scotland. Its Ailsa golf course is especially well renowned.

✉ Maidens Road, on the A719 ☎ 01655 331000; www.turnberryresort.co.uk

RESTAURANTS

GLASGOW
The Buttery (£££)
More of an experience than a restaurant. Step through the door into this remnant of old world elegance and sample some of the finest cooking in Scotland.

✉ 652 Argyle Street ☎ 0141 221 8188

Café Hula (£–££)
See page 58.

City Merchant (£–££)
A favourite here for 20 years, this family-run restaurant serves good Scottish produce in warm surroundings. The emphasis is on Scottish specialities – try the seafood platter or a perfectly hung steak.

✉ 97 Candleriggs ☎ 0141 553 1577

Stravaigan (££)
A big favourite with locals, this gastro-pub par excellence uses fine Scottish ingredients in its imaginative and eclectic menu. Expect the likes of fish and shellfish in a Thai coconut and ginger broth.

✉ 28 Gibson Street ☎ 0141 334 2665

La Parmigiana (££)

Locals, who should know a good deal, have supported this trattoria for years. The baked sea bass with a lemon butter sauce is tasty, as are the classic Italian dishes.

✉ 447 Great Western Road ☎ 0141 334 0686

78 St Vincent Street (£–££)

See page 59.

Ubiquitous Chip (£–££)

Wonderful, popular restaurant and bistro. The Scottish menu is served in the courtyard restaurant or in the upstairs balcony.

✉ 12 Ashton Lane, Hillhead ☎ 0141 334 5007

AYR
Fouters Bistro (£–££)

New owners George Ramage and Tom Harwood are continuing the 30-year tradition of modern Scottish cooking at Fouters, one of the most popular eating places in the west of Scotland.

✉ 2A Academy Street ☎ 01292 261391

DUMFRIES
Hullabaloo Restaurant (££)

See page 59.

GATEHOUSE OF FLEET
The Masonic Arms (£–££)

Three rooms, each with its individual atmosphere, serve up a fine selection of local fish and beef. Pretty conservatory for summer.

✉ 10 Ann Street ☎ 01557 814335

MAYBOLE
Wildings Restaurant (££)

Consistently good fish and seafood restaurant right near Girvan Harbour. Good specialities include tempura prawns and home-made fishcakes, extensive wine list.

✉ Harbour Road, Maidens, near Maybole ☎ 01655 331401

MOFFAT
Lime Tree Restaurant (££)
There's good food at sensible prices in this popular restaurant, recently relocated from the town centre to a guest house on the edge of town. Traditional and modern Scottish cooking using local, seasonal ingredients.

✉ Hartfell House, Hartfell Crescent ☎ 01683 220153

MONIAIVE
Craigdarroch Arms (£)
This very old hotel has a good reputation for its food. Ranging from bar snacks to a full restaurant menu with such delights as pan-seared ostrich steaks and the famed Craigdarroch mixed grill.

✉ High Street ☎ 01848 200205

NEWTON STEWART
Kirroughtree House (£££)
Duck with potatoes, celeriac purée, black pudding and ratatouille may sound like a terrible mixture but just wait till you see how they are combined to create one of the dishes for which the hotel is famous.

✉ Newton Stewart ☎ 01671 402141

PORTPATRICK
Campbell's (££)
Deservedly popular, this family-run restaurant serves superb fish and shellfish. Try the crab and lobster fished from the family boat as well as well-hung meat from local producers.

✉ 1 South Crescent ☎ 01776 810314

TROON
MacCallums of Troon Oyster Bar (££–£££)
A low-key, harbourside building in Troon is the setting for this excellent fish eatery, considered by many Glaswegians to be worth the journey out from the city. Excellent fish and chip shop next door.

✉ The Harbour ☎ 01292 319339

TURNBERRY
Westin Turnberry Resort Hotel (£££)
Treat yourself to a meal here, or perhaps afternoon tea on the Terrace Brasserie.

✉ Just north of the village on the A719 ☎ 01655 331000

SHOPPING

CRAFTS AND GIFT SHOPS
Octopus Crafts
A beautiful selection of hand-made artisan gifts, crafts and cookware is on offer at this farm complex outside Fairlie village – try the restaurant too.

✉ Fencefoot Farm, Fairlie, near Largs ☎ 01475 568918

FASHION
Felix and Oscar
This West End Glasgow store, going for over 10 years, is the place to track down funky and original clothes and accessories as well as products from names such as Cath Kidston, Orla Kiely and Trousselier.

✉ 459 Great Western Road, Glasgow ☎ 0141 339 8585

Princes Square
This up-market mall in Glasgow has the pick of the bunch fashion- and beauty-wise, as well as gifts and home-wares.

✉ 48 Buchanan Street, Galsgow ☎ 0141 221 0342;
www.princessquare.co.uk

BOOKS
Border Books
Get lost for hours, even days, in this enormous literary emporium.

✉ 98 Buchanan Street, Glasgow ☎ 0141 222 7700

Voltaire & Rousseau
This is the longest running second-hand book shop in Glasgow and an absolute must see for anyone interested in books.

✉ 12–14 Otago Lane, Glasgow ☎ 0141 339 1811

WHISKY
Auchentoshan Distillery
Glasgow's own malt whisky distillery offers guided tours and tastings and the full range of its whisky products in the shop.
✉ A82 by Dalmuir ☎ 01389 878561

FOOD AND DRINK
Galloway Lodge Preserves
Limited-edition, home-made jams, chutneys, preserves, pickles and mustards are sold here alongside some of the best of Scotland's designer pottery.
✉ Burgh Lodge, Gatehouse of Fleet ☎ 01557 814007

Peckhams
Amazing deli stocking a wide range of Scottish produce, and open until late. Just the place for a spot of last-minute shopping before you leave. The Edinburgh branch is at Waverley station.
✉ 61–65 Glassford Street, Glasgow ☎ 0141 553 0666; www.peckhams.co.uk

ENTERTAINMENT

GLASGOW
The Citizens
This is one of the most influential theatres in Europe, with a magnificent, recently renovated auditorium. If you only visit one theatre while you are in Scotland, make it this one.
✉ 119 Gorbals Street ☎ 0141 429 0022; www.citz.co.uk

Carling Academy Glasgow
This new live music venue, housed in what was once an art-deco cinema, hosts excellent cutting edge live acts.
✉ 121 Eglinton Street, Glasgow ☎ 0141 418 3000;
www.glasgow-academy.co.uk

Barrowland
This iconic live music venue is renowned for its great sprung dance floor, ideal the enthusiasm of its eclectic, full-on audiences.
✉ 244 Gallowgate, Glasgow ☎ 0141 552 4601

King Tut's Wah Wah Hut
Live music is played most nights with local and national bands and the occasional very big name.

✉ 272a St Vincent Street ☎ 0141 221 5279; www.kingtuts.co.uk

Royal Concert Hall
Hugely successful, with one of the most widely ranging concert performances in Britain from classical to jazz.

✉ 2 Sauchiehall Street ☎ 0141 353 8000; www.grch.com

The Scotia Bar
See page 70.

The Tron
Trendy and contemporary restaurant, bar and theatre.

✉ 63 Trongate ☎ 0141 552 4267; www.tron.co.uk

Victoria Bar
See page 70.

SPORT

Allander Sports Complex
Great family venue with pool, badminton, snooker and squash.

✉ Milngavie Road, Bearsden, Glasgow ☎ 0141 942 2233

Scotstoun Leisure Centre
Multi-sports complex, including swimming pool and soccer.

✉ Danes Drive, Glasgow ☎ 0141 276 1620; www.csglasgow.org

Time Capsule
A short drive from the city centre, this combined pool and ice rink, with other leisure facilities thrown in, is a great hit with families.

✉ 100 Buchanan Street, Coatbridge, Glasgow ☎ 01236 449572

Magnum Leisure Centre
Huge place with leisure pool, ice rink, squash, bowls and more.

✉ Irvine Harbour, Irvine ☎ 01294 278381

Dundee and Central Scotland

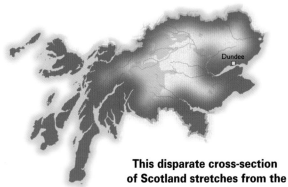

This disparate cross-section of Scotland stretches from the lonely island-scattered western coastline of Argyll and the Hebrides to the fishing villages of the East Neuk of Fife on the Firth of Forth, all the way to the silvery Tay, the city of Dundee, Angus and the North Sea beyond. It includes wild hills, moorlands and waterways, the bustling small towns of Scotland's central belt and lush agricultural land.

Rising in the great central plain is Stirling Castle, which saw fierce fighting in the Scottish Wars of Independence (1296–1328), while further north lie the refined country town of Perth, down-to-earth Dundee and the glorious heather-covered Angus Glens.

DUNDEE

Dundee straggles untidily along the River Tay, its two distinctive bridges reaching out long thin highways of road and rail over the broad stretch of water to Fife. Of the three Js – jute, jam and journalism – which were the lifeblood of the town, only journalism remains, in the shape of DC Thomson, who publish the *Dandy* and *Beano* comics and the *Sunday Post*. In the surrounding countryside, the berry fields which supplied the jam factories now allow you to pick your own fruit. The town has reinvented itself as a popular conference venue, helped by the unassuming friendliness of the people. This, together with the unpretentious cultural life, excellent museums, including the interactive Sensation Science Centre, and small theatres, make it an agreeable base for touring the area.

www.angusanddundee.co.uk

✚ 20G

Broughty Ferry and Castle

Broughty Ferry, once a separate village, is now a suburb of Dundee. It is popular with Dundonians and visitors alike, with its eclectic mix of restaurants, pubs and shops and sandy beach along the banks of the Tay. Fifteenth-century **Broughty Castle,** now a museum, tells the story of Broughty Ferry and the whaling industry.

Broughty Castle

☎ 01382 436916 🕓 Mon–Sat 10–4, Sun 12:30–4; closed Mon Oct–Mar 🖐 Free

RRS *Discovery* and HM Frigate *Unicorn*

Once the pride of the Panmuir yard, where it was built in 1901 for the polar expeditions of Captain Robert Falcon Scott, the **Royal Research Ship *Discovery*** lay rotting for years on London's Thames Embankment. Finally, the ship was restored and returned to its birthplace. Now housed at the specially designed Discovery Point, it has become a major tourist attraction.

The Frigate *Unicorn*, further along the Tay at Victoria Dock, is the oldest British warship still afloat. Built in 1824, it was, incredibly, still in service until 1968.

RRS *Discovery*

✉ Victoria Quay, near the Tay Bridge
☎ 01382 309060; www.rrsdiscovery.com
🕐 Apr–Sep Mon–Sat 10–6, Sun 11–6; Oct–Mar Mon–Sat 10–5, Sun 11–5
✋ Expensive 🍴 Café (£)

McManus Art Gallery and Museum

This is a gem of a place, one of the finest Victorian buildings in Dundee, and that's just the outside. Indoors, the museum covers Dundee's history from the ancient Picts to modern times. There's also a great display on the Tay Bridge disaster. On 28 December, 1879, the bridge collapsed in a storm after only 18 months, and 75 people died. Upstairs in the Albert Hall, with its pitch pine-panelled roof, are collections of glass, gold, silver, musical instruments and furniture, including the table where death warrants for captured Jacobites were signed after the Battle of Culloden in 1746. The Victoria Gallery has Scottish collections and superb Pre-Raphaelites.
www.mcmanus.co.uk

✉ Albert Square ☎ 01382 432350 🕐 Closed for renovation at the time of writing; expected to reopen by 2010 💰 Free 🍴 Café (£)

Mills Observatory

This is the only full-time public observatory in Britain, and offers guided tours. There are special openings for eclipses and the odd visiting comet. Winter evenings are the best time to go, but in the summer, when it's light, there are good exhibits and displays.
www.dundeecity.gov.uk/mills

✉ Balgay Park. Approach via Perth Road, Blackness Avenue, Balgay Road
☎ 01382 435967 🕐 Apr–Sep Tue–Fri 11–5, Sat, Sun 12:30–4; Oct–Mar Mon–Fri 4–10, Sat, Sun 12:30–4 💰 Free

🍴 Light refreshments (£)
❓ Reservations essential for large groups and for Planetarium

Verdant Works

Verdant Works was one of Dundee's many jute mills which produced hessian and sacking, and once employed 50,000 people locally; it has been restored and reconstructed as a museum. Volunteers operate textile machines, while 'Juteopolis', a 15-minute film, explains the impact of the industry on the city and its people. Every day at 1pm the works' 'bummer' (whistle) is blown, a sound that marked the livelihood of many families and recalls its history in an evocative way. Guided tours are available.
www.verdantworks.com

✉ 27 West Henderson's Wynd ☎ 01382 309060 🕐 Apr–Oct Mon–Sat 10–5, Sun 11–6; Nov–Mar Wed–Sat 10:30–4:30, Sun 11–4:30 💰 Expensive 🍴 Refreshments (£)

a drive around Central Scotland

Start from Perth. Take the A85, then turn right on to the A93 and right again on to the A94. (Scone Palace, ➤ 143, is 2.5km/1.5 miles further along the A93.) At Balbeggie, take the B953 to Inchture, then turn left on to the A90. Take the A85 right through Dundee, past Discovery Point and follow the signs for the Tay Bridge and the A92. Pass through Newport-on-Tay and Leuchars to St Andrews, then follow the A917. Follow the coastline of the East Neuk, diverting through the picturesque villages of Crail, Anstruther, Pittenweem, St Monane and Elie.

From Crail take the B940 to Scotland's Secret Bunker. This underground relic of the Cold War would have become the administrative centre of Scotland in the event of a nuclear attack. It was an official secret until 1994 when it opened to the public. Part of it is still operational.

Turn left on to the A915.

Have a look at Lower Largo, with its statue of Alexander Selkirk, the inspiration for Robinson Crusoe. A native of Largo, Selkirk ran away to sea and was marooned on Juan Fernand Island from 1705 to 1709.

Continue on the A915, then turn right on to the A911 and in Glenrothes turn right on to the A92, then left on to the A912. At Falkland follow the B936 to Auchtermuchty and turn left on to the A91. From the A91 turn left on to the B919, left on to the A911, then after Kinnesswood, right on to the B920. At the intersection turn right on to the

*B9097, right again on to the B996 and continue
to Kinross.*

This route circles Loch Leven with the 14th-century ruins of
Loch Leven Castle on an island. Mary, Queen of Scots, was
imprisoned here in 1567.

*Take the A922 to Milnathort and the B996 via Glenfarg
to the A912. Turn left and follow the road through Bridge
of Earn back to Perth.*

Distance 190km (118 miles)
Time 6–8 hours including stops
Start/end point Perth ✚ 19H
Lunch The Naafi at the Secret Bunker (£) ☎ 01333 310301

Central Scotland

THE ANGUS GLENS

The Glens of Angus are a series of five glorious glens, rich in flora and fauna. Of particular interest are the red deer and Arctic plants. Glen Clova is the most picturesque of the glens, offering several lovely walks. Jock's Road, leading through the mountains to Braemar, some 22.5km (14 miles) away, is spectacular. The path clings, precariously at times, to the hill's edge, the water runs far below and, as you climb, the view of the glen behind falls away in a changing, winding perspective, misty in the distance. Beware, this is passable only in summer.

✚ 9F

BO'NESS AND KINNEIL RAILWAY

This is one of the best small independent railway lines and the largest collection of vintage trains in Scotland. The track from Bo'ness leads 5km/3 miles to Birkhill, where you can visit the Birkhill Clay Mine or stroll in the Avon Gorge before the old steam train departs for the return trip.
www.srps.org.uk

➕ 19J ✉ Off Union Street, Bo'ness ☎ 01506
822298 ✋ Apr–Oct every weekend (Jul–Aug
Tue–Sun); Santa Specials Dec weekends
✋ Moderate

CRARAE GARDEN

Between Inveraray and Lochgilphead, this National Trust garden is
laid out around the glen of the Crarae Burn which flows into Loch
Fyne. Covering around 25ha (62 acres), there are two walking
routes, the inner and outer circles that both start from the car park.
Strategically placed seats allow you to enjoy majestic views over
Loch Fyne while admiring the snowdrops, daffodils, bluebells,
azaleas, rhododendrons or magnolias, depending on the season.
www.nts.org.uk

➕ 16H ✉ A83, 16km (10 miles) southwest of Inveraray ☎ 01546 886614
✋ Gardens daily dawn–dusk; visitor centre Apr–Oct daily 10–5 ✋ Moderate
🍴 Refreshments (£)

CULROSS AND CULROSS PALACE

The National Trust for Scotland tends the red-tiled houses and
whitewashed walls of this delightful town. Walk through the
cobbled Back Causeway, visit the remains of the Cistercian
Culross Abbey, or the Study, a restored 17th-century house.
The 16th-century merchant's house known as **Culross Palace**
is the main attraction, with little rooms and narrow passages.
St Mungo, the founder, and
patron saint of Glasgow, was
reputedly born here.

➕ 19H ✉ 12km (7.5 miles) west of
Dunfermline

Culross Palace
☎ 01383 880359; www.nts.org.uk
🕐 Apr–Sep daily 12–5 ✋ Moderate
🍴 Café (£)

EAST NEUK OF FIFE

The coastline of the East Neuk is dotted with a string of little fishing villages. Quaint cottages with red-tiled roofs and crow-stepped gables perch around secluded harbours. Crail is the prettiest, while Anstruther and Pittenweem are regular working ports. Anstruther is home to the **Scottish Fisheries Museum,** where the entire history of fishing in Scotland unfolds. Kellie Castle, north of Anstruther, is a restored 16th-century building with a garden full of nooks and crannies.

✚ 21H

Scottish Fisheries Museum

✉ Anstruther Harbour

☎ 01333 310628;
www.scotfishmuseum.org

🕔 Apr–Sep Mon–Sat 10–5:30, Sun 11–5;
Oct–Mar Mon–Sat 10–4:30, Sun 12–4:30

✋ Moderate

🍴 Tea room (£)

THE FALKIRK WHEEL

Designed to connect the Forth and Clyde and Union canals, this massive rotating boat lift carries eight boats at a time. The state-of-the-art visitor centre tells the story of the wheel and the history of canals. Boat trips from the centre sail on to the wheel which ascends to join the Union Canal 35m (115ft) above. The journey continues along the canal by the Antonine Wall before returning.
www.thefalkirkwheeel.co.uk

✚ 19J ✉ Lime Road, Tamfourhill, Falkirk ☎ 08700 500208 🕔 Visitor centre Apr–Oct daily 9:30–6; Nov–Mar Mon–Wed 11–3, Thu–Sun 10–4:30
✋ Visitor centre free; boat trip expensive

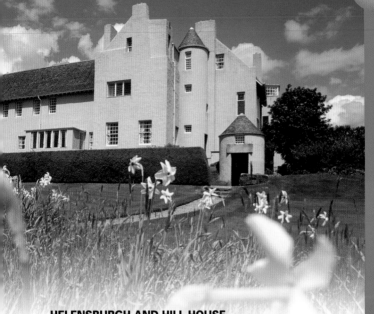

HELENSBURGH AND HILL HOUSE

The main attraction in this attractive Georgian town on the Firth of Clyde is **Hill House,** designed by Charles Rennie Mackintosh in 1902 for the publisher Walter Blackie. Mackintosh was given a completely free hand in the design of the house, its interior and furnishings. The result is one of the finest art nouveau houses in Britain, now painstakingly restored by The National Trust for Scotland. The exterior echoes a traditional tower with its irregular windows, round turret and solid expanses of wall. Inside, it is light and elegant with perfect proportions and delightful glimpses of the adjoining spaces as you move through it.

Henry Bell, the inventor of the *Comet*, an early steam-driven boat, was swimming instructor in Helensburgh, which was also the birthplace of the inventor of television, John Logie Baird.

✚ 17J

Hill House

✉ Upper Colquhoun Street ☎ 01436 673900; www.nts.org.uk ⏰ Apr–Oct daily 1:30–5:30 👣 Expensive 🍴 Tea room (£)

THE INNER HEBRIDES

There's a magical quality about the islands of Islay, Jura, Mull, Iona, Coll and Tiree. Most tourists head for Tobermory on Mull, with its bright houses fronting the harbour where, tradition has it, the wreck of a Spanish galleon lies laden with gold. Iona, with its mighty cathedral and connections with St Columba, draws pilgrims from all over the world. Jura has wonderful, blindingly white, sandy beaches that are all but deserted – just the spot to get away from it all. But it is to Islay that you must go if you want to experience some of the finest whiskies in Scotland. Islay malts are unique and easily distinguished by their smokey, peaty taste.

✚ 3F

INVERARAY

This small 18th-century town, built by the Duke of Argyll, clan chief of the Campbells, has an enchanting view over Loch Fyne. The old gaol and adjoining courthouse are now a museum. Inveraray Castle, home of the Duke of Argyll, would not

be out of place on the Loire. In the stable block the Combined Operations Museum is dedicated to the troops that trained on Loch Fyne for the D-Day landings in Normandy. Inside the castle itself is a collection of weapons given to the Campbells by the government to help repress the Jacobites.

Southwest of Inveraray is the restored township of **Auchindrain,** now a folk museum, with around 20 thatched cottages set up to re-create life prior to the Clearances (▶ 153).

✚ 17H

Auchindrain
✉ 10km (6 miles) southwest of Inveraray ☎ 01499 500235; www.auchindrainmuseum.org.uk 🕓 Apr–Oct daily 10–5 ✋ Moderate

KIRRIEMUIR

Kirriemuir was the birthplace of J M Barrie, novelist, dramatist and creator of *Peter Pan*. The house he was born in is a **museum,** and outside is the wash house: the prototype of the house the Lost Boys built for Wendy, which the young Barrie used as a theatre for his first plays. Barrie is buried in the local cemetery.

✚ 9F

J M Barrie's Birthplace
✉ 9 Brechin Road ☎ 01575 572646; www.nts.org.uk 🕓 Jul–Aug daily 12–5; Apr–Jun, Sep–Oct Fri–Wed 12–5 ✋ Moderate

LINLITHGOW

Mary, Queen of Scots, was born here at **Linlithgow Palace** in 1542. Although a royal building had existed here since the time of David I (1124–53), it was James I who built the present one. It survived until 1746 when it was destroyed by fire, but it's well worth a visit. Overlooking Linlithgow Loch, the roofless ruin has spiral staircases, stately rooms, a magnificent Great Hall, and a brewery down below.

✚ 19J

Linlithgow Palace

✉ South shore of loch ☎ 01506 842896; www.historic-scotland.gov.uk
🕐 Apr–Sep daily 9:30–5:30; Oct–Mar 9:30–4:30 ✋ Moderate

LOCH AWE

This is the longest freshwater loch in Scotland. There are forest walks at Barnaline, near Dalavich, and near the head of the loch you will find the tiny island of Inishail, with its 13th-century chapel. At Taynuilt, visit the restored industrial heritage centre of **Bonawe Iron Furnace** before heading back towards the loch via the gloomy Pass of Brander for a tour of the Cruachan Power Station. The

station is built into Ben Cruachan, where hydroelectricity is generated by water pumped up the mountain from the loch below.

➕ 17H

Bonawe Iron Furnace

✉ Off the A85 at Bonawe ☎ 01866 822432; www.historic-scotland.gov.uk
🕐 Mar–Sep daily 9:30–5:30 ✋ Moderate

LOCH LOMOND

Loch Lomond and the Trossachs together form a National Park (➤ 147). Easily accessible, the loch can be overcrowded during the tourist season, but it is a great beauty spot. To escape the crowds, take one of the many boat trips from Balloch which head round the small islands on the loch, or follow the West Highland Way on the east bank to Balmaha and Rowardennan. From here, a path climbs up Ben Lomond, 972m (3,188ft), with sweeping views from the top across the Southern Highlands.

➕ 18H ℹ National Park Gateway Centre ✉ Ben Lomond Way, Loch Lomond Shores, Balloch ☎ 08707 200607; www.visitscottishheartlands.com and www.lochlomond-trossachs.org 🕐 Aug daily 9–6:30; Sep 10–6; Oct, Apr–May 10–5:30; Nov–Mar 10–5; Jun 9.30–6

MONTROSE BASIN WILDLIFE CENTRE

The Basin, a huge tidal lagoon of mud, is a rich habitat for all manner of wildlife. Humans may hold their noses but to the geese, waders and swans that frequent the basin, grubbing in the smelly mud is a gourmet experience. Telescopes, video cameras and binoculars are strategically placed to enable visitors to watch without disturbing the birds, and there is a series of guided walks led by the resident ranger.
www.swt.org.uk

🚻 10F ✉ 1.5km (1 mile) from Montrose, on the A92 ☎ 01674 676336 🕐 Reserve summer 8–8, winter dawn–dusk. Visitor centre 15 Mar–15 Nov daily 10–5; 16 Nov–14 Mar Fri–Sun 10:30–4
✋ Inexpensive

OBAN

Oban, the main terminal for Caledonian MacBrayne Ferries, is known as the gateway to the Isles. On a hill above, McCaig's Folly, a Colosseum look-alike built to give employment to returning soldiers, dominates the town, harbour and bay. Outside the town are the ruins of 13th-century **Dunstaffnage Castle,** where Flora MacDonald was imprisoned after helping Bonnie Prince Charlie in his escape. The Isle of Kerrera in Oban Bay, with a population of less than 50, is easily reached by ferry. It is a peaceful retreat with great views over to Mull and Colonsay.

✚ 16G

Dunstaffnage Castle

✉ 5km (3 miles) north of Oban, off the A85

☎ 01631 562465; www.historic-scotland.gov.uk

🕐 Apr–Sep daily 9:30–5:30 (4:30 Oct); Nov–Mar
Sat–Wed 9:30–4:30 💷 Inexpensive

PERTH

Perth is a prosperous market town in the
heart of rich farmlands. Visit the Victorian
water-driven oat mill at Lower City Mills and
the cobbled streets around it. Bell's
Cherrybank Gardens has Britain's largest
collection of heathers and a super children's
play area. At the Caithness Glass factory see
glass blown in the traditional way.

Scone, just to the north, where all the
monarchs of Scotland were crowned on the
Stone of Destiny, is the historic heart of
Scotland. Ancient **Scone Palace** was
restored and extended in the 19th century
and this elegant Gothic mansion is home to
the Earl of Mansfield. The grounds, house
and history are fascinating, but there is also
an extraordinary collection of furniture,
porcelain, delicate ivories, and papier mâché
that once belonged to Louis XV of France.

✚ 19H

Scone Palace

✉ Off the A93 Braemar Road, 3km (2 miles)
northeast of Perth ☎ 01738 552300; www.scone-
palace.co.uk 🕐 Apr–Oct 9:30–5:30; last admission
5; grounds open until 5:45 💷 Expensive

🍴 Restaurant (££) and coffee shop (£)

PITLOCHRY

Pitlochry is a popular tourist town on the banks of the River Tummel, where the Blair Athol Distillery has been making its famous malt since 1798. The power station produces electricity from the artificially created Loch Faskally, and the salmon ladder to help the fish negotiate the dam is a sight not to be missed. Pitlochry Festival Theatre is famous for its productions. Enjoy a backstage tour during the day and return in the evening for a performance of the latest play.

Near the town is the **Pass of Killiecrankie,** site of the famous Battle of Killicrankie in 1689 where the Jacobites, led by Graham of Claverhouse (Bonnie Dundee), defeated the government forces, although Dundee himself was killed. This deep wooded gorge has a visitor centre with exhibits on the gorge and the battle.

✚ 8F

Pass of Killiecrankie

✉ Off the A9, 5km (3 miles) north of Pitlochry ☎ 01796 473233; www.nts.org.uk ⚕ Site open all year. Visitor centre Apr–Oct daily 10–5:30 Free 🍴 Snack bar (£)

ST ANDREWS

Scotland's oldest university town is world famous as the home of golf, which has been played here since the 15th century. The Royal and Ancient Golf Club is the governing body of the sport and in 1873 the first British Open Championship was held here. The **British Golf Museum** is the best there is, with lots of hands-on stuff and plenty

of history. However, if golf is not your scene take a walk around the historic streets to the ruins of the great cathedral, once the largest in Scotland. It was consecrated in 1318 in the presence of King Robert the Bruce and destroyed in 1559 by supporters of John Knox. An impressive ruin, it is particularly beautiful at twilight in half silhouette.

✚ 20H

British Golf Museum

✉ Bruce Embankment, opposite the Royal and Ancient Golf Club ☎ 01334 460046; www.britishgolfmuseum.co.uk 🕐 Apr–Oct daily 9:30–5, Sun 10–5; Nov–Mar 10–4 ✋ Moderate

STIRLING

Stirling Castle, like Edinburgh Castle, is perched atop the plug of an extinct volcano, but in many ways Stirling is more dramatic. Surrounded by a wide plain, the castle is the most prominent sight for miles around and in past times the narrow bridge here was a strategic gateway between North and South. Many of the decisive battles in Scotland's history, including Stirling Bridge (1297) and Bannockburn (1314) were fought around here. At the Lady's Rock in the cemetery there is a pointer to all the surrounding battle sites. Bannockburn's visitor centre details the battle in an excellent audiovisual presentation. The Wallace Monument high on the cliffs overlooking the site of the Battle of Stirling Bridge contains the hero's massive two-handed sword.

✚ 19H
Stirling Castle
✉ Castle Wynd ☎ 01786 450000 🕐 Apr–Sep
daily 9:30–6; Oct–Mar 9:30–5 ✋ Expensive
🍴 Café (£)

THE TROSSACHS NATIONAL PARK

Together with Loch Lomond (▶ 141), the
Trossachs form Scotland's first National Park.
This wild countryside of moors, hills and
forests, from Loch Katrine to Loch Lomond,
was the haunt of Rob Roy MacGregor – outlaw,
cattle thief, murderer or hero depending on your
point of view. He died at a ripe old age in his
own bed and is buried in the beautiful
churchyard at Balquhidder. The Trossachs is the
largest area of wilderness in central Scotland,
with excellent walking, climbing and fishing and
the spectacular scenery. If you can't make it to
the Highlands, this is as near as you'll get to the

majestic scale of the north. Its
position right at the heart of
Scotland means that it is easily
accessible and very popular.

Main towns in the area are
Callander and Aberfoyle.
www.lochlomond-trossachs.org
✚ 18H 🛈 Trossachs Discovery
Centre ✉ Main Street, Aberfoyle
☎ 08707 200604;
www.visitscottishheartlands.com
🕐 Apr–Oct daily, Nov–Mar
Sat–Sun. Many tourist information
offices; check website for nearest

HOTELS

ARDUAINE
Loch Melfort Hotel (££)
Glorious views over Loch Melfort and down the Sound of Jura, combined with excellent cuisine using the best local produce.
✉ On the A816 midway between Oban and Lochgilphead ☎ 01852 200233; www.lochmelfort.co.uk

AUCHTERARDER
The Gleneagles Hotel (£££)
Beautiful countryside, outstanding range of activities and first-class cuisine make this one of the world's top hotels.
✉ On the A823 ☎ 01764 662231; www.gleneagles.com

CRAIL
Balcomie Links (£–££)
Friendly, good-value, family-run hotel near the golf course in Fife's most picturesque coastal village.
✉ Balcomie Road ☎ 01333 450237; www.balcomie.co.uk

CRIEFF
Knock Castle Hotel (££–£££)
Stay in this 19th-century baronial castle to enjoy peace, comfort and pampering. Beautiful views and a good restaurant.
✉ Drummond Terrace ☎ 01764 650088; www.knockcastle.com

DUNDEE
The Apex City Quay (££–£££)
This sleek, modern hotel, right on the waterfront, is the best place to stay in Dundee. Offers a wide range of services and facilities.
✉ West Victoria Dock Road ☎ 01382 202404; www.apexhotels.co.uk

KILLIECRANKIE
Killiecrankie (££)
A 19th-century country manse overlooking the River Garry and the historic Pass of Killiecrankie. Close to Blair Castle and Pitlochry.
✉ West of Killiecrankie on the B8079 ☎ 01796 473220

PERTH
The Royal George (££)
A Georgian hotel, with a small garden overlooking the river. A good mix of locals and tourists in the bars and restaurants.

✉ Tay Street ✉ 01738 624455; www.theroyalgeorgehotel.co.uk

ST ANDREWS
The Old Course Hotel (£££)
Situated as close to the 17th hole of the world's most famous golf course as you can get without playing it.

✉ St Andrews ☎ 01334 474371; www.oldcoursehotel.kohler.com

TAYNUILT
Ardanaiseig Hotel (£££)
One of Scotland's top country house hotels, this Gothic mansion is set in landscaped grounds overlooking the water.

✉ Kilchrenan ☎ 01866 833333; www.ardnaiseig.com

TOBERMORY, ISLE OF MULL
Western Isles Hotel (££)
Overlooking Tobermory Bay, this hotel has superb views.

✉ Above the town ☎ 01688 302012; www.mullhotel.com

RESTAURANTS

ANSTRUTHER
Cellar Restaurant (££)
This used to be a cooperage where barrels were made for the herring industry. Now herrings are served to the customers along with a wide variety of other fish, East Neuk crab and meat.

✉ 24 East Green ☎ 01333 310378

ARDUAINE
Loch Melfort Hotel (£££)
Sit in the dining room gazing out over Loch Melfort while you wait for your food – splendid fare based on local seafood.

✉ On the A816 midway between Oban and Lochgilphead ☎ 01852 200233; www.lochmelfort.co.uk

AUCHTERARDER
The Gleneagles Hotel (£££)
Soufflé created from Lanark blue cheese and pine nuts, chargrilled quail and smoked venison are just a few of the dishes here.

✉ On A823 ☎ 01764 662231

BALQUHIDDER
Monachyle Mhor (££)
Good food served in a dining room overlooking two lochs.

✉ Off the A84, south of Lochearnhead ☎ 01877 384622

BLAIR ATHOLL
The Loft (£)
There are all the usual bistro favourites on the lunch and evening menus of this friendly restaurant, served upstairs in a converted loft. Excellent steaks and good value.

✉ Blair Atholl ☎ 01796 481377

OBAN
The Seafood Temple (£)
Some of the best-value oysters and lobsters in Scotland are on offer at this laid-back, relaxed eating house outside Oban.

✉ Gallanack Road ☎ 01631 560000

PERTH
Deans at Let's Eat (£££)
Modern Scottish dishes such as Blairgowrie beef fillet medallion.

✉ 77–79 Kinnoull Street ☎ 01738 643377

63 Tay Street (££–£££)
In an imposing building overlooking the River Tay with wood floors and white walls. Modern menu with classical roots.

✉ 63 Tay Street ☎ 01738 441451

PITLOCHRY
The Old Armoury (£££)
This cosy yet airy restaurant serves locally sourced meat and

freshwater fish, carefully cooked with fresh vegetables. Good puddings and Scottish cheeses. Garden for summer eating. The set menus are good value.

✉ Armoury Road ☎ 01796 474281

ST ANDREWS
The Grange Inn (££)
Set above the town with lovely coastal views, the Grange has a long reputation as a gastropub par excellence. Pretty interior, nice garden and good range of Scottish and imaginative dishes.

✉ Grange Road ☎ 01334 472670

Peat Inn (£££)
David Wilson has made the Peat Inn, near St Andrews, a watchword for superb cuisine; it is the best place to eat in Fife.

✉ 10km (6 miles) southwest of St Andrews at intersection of the B940/B941
☎ 01334 840206; www.thepeatinn.co.uk

The Seafood Restaurant (££–£££)
A stunning waterside glass pavilion houses St Andrews' best restaurant, where you can enjoy innovative, contemporary cuisine using the finest of local ingredients. Good value set menu and some meat dishes.

✉ Bruce Embankment ☎ 01334 479475

STIRLING
L'Angevine (£–££)
Ideally situated near Stirling Castle, this Scottish-French bistro serves food reflecting both cultures in generous portions.

✉ 52 Spittal Street ☎ 01786 446124

TAYNUILT
Taychreggan Hotel (£££)
This former drovers' inn on Loch Awe now serves great Scottish food in a special fixed-price, five-course menu with at least three choices of main course.

✉ From the A85 take the B845 at Taynuilt ☎ 01866 833211

SHOPPING

CRAFTS AND GIFT SHOPS

Crail Pottery

This pottery is crammed with delights in plain and brightly coloured glazed earthenware – vases, bowls, pitchers, oven-to-table ware and lovely planters for the garden.

✉ 75 Nethergate, Crail ☎ 01333 451222; www.crailpottery.com

Crieff Visitor Centre

Offers a wide selection of ceramics and Caithness glass.

✉ Muthill Road, Crieff ☎ 01764 654014; www.crieff.co.uk

House of Bruar

The ultimate Highland shopping experience offers everything from high-end art through a superb food hall to cashmere, tweeds and outdoor clothing – a must-stop on the A9 north.

✉ Bruar, by Pitlochry ☎ 01796 483236; www.houseofbruar.com

MacNaughton's

One of Scotland's best one-stop tweed, wool and tartan treasure houses, this huge store has its own woollen mills and a fantastic selection of Scottish textiles – with wonderful tartan goodies.

✉ Station Road, Pitlochry ☎ 01796 472722; www.macnaughtonsofpitlochry.com

ENTERTAINMENT

MacRobert Arts Centre

Excellent venue on university campus for live theatre, mainstream and art-house cinema, live jazz and dance.

✉ MacRoberts Arts Centre, Stirling ☎ 01786 466666; www.macrobert.org

Mull Little Theatre

Now in a larger, specially built premises just outside Tobermory.

✉ Druimfin, Mull ☎ 01688 302828; www.mulltheatre.com

The Taybank

See page 71.

Aberdeen and the North

The Highlands and Islands are the Scotland of literature, romance and the movies, a vast area, much of it unforgiving mountain or natural moorland. On the east coast is Aberdeen – the granite city.

Aberdeen

Many species of wildlife which have disappeared elsewhere survive in the scarcely populated wildernesses here. Scattered ruined cottages remain, testimony to a more populous past before the Clearances in the 18th and 19th centuries, when the landlords drove the people from the land in favour of more profitable sheep.

Highlanders emigrated in droves to the New World, taking with them their oral traditions of music and storytelling and their memories of the land they left behind. Exiled Scots and their descendants get very nostalgic at the mention of misty glens, heather-covered hillsides and dark deep lochs. It is easy to mock, but travel this land once and you will understand how they feel.

ABERDEEN

Aberdeen, the grey granite city of the North, is the hub of Scotland's oil industry, a thriving fishing port and home to one of the four ancient universities of Scotland. Surprisingly, for the most northerly city of Scotland, it is famed for its prolific gardens. The nightlife is lively on account of the university and the prosperity of its cosmopolitan population. Understanding the language, however, can present problems and a crash course in the Doric, the local dialect, might be a good idea. In the meantime, to the standard greeting 'Fit like?', simply answer 'Nae bad, foo's yersel?' Translated it means 'How are you?', 'Not bad, how are you?'

➕ 11E

www.aberdeen-grampian.com

Aberdeen Maritime Museum

The 1593 Provost Ross's house, one of the oldest buildings in the city, is home to this remarkable museum that tells the story of Aberdeen's maritime heritage. Everything is covered, from herring fishing and whaling to ship-building and the late 20th-century oil industry. The ancient rooms combine with state-of-the-art

computers, audiovisual technology, objects and oral history.
www.aagm.co.uk

✉ 52 Shiprow ☎ 01224 213066 🕐 Mon–Sat 10–5, Sun 12–3 ✋ Moderate

Fish Market and Harbour

Fishing is still one of the mainstays of the local economy and few
sights can compare with the bustling harbour where fishing
vessels lie alongside oil-rig supply boats and modern cruise liners.
Pay an early morning visit to the fish market to mingle with the
buyers and fishermen as thousands of tons of freshly landed fish
are bid for then loaded into huge refrigerated trucks to be
transported throughout the UK.

Provost Skene's House

Dating from 1545, Aberdeen's
oldest private dwelling house
was the home of its provost
(mayor), Sir George Skene, from
1676 to 1685, and is preserved
almost unchanged. Astonishingly,
its luminous religious paintings
survived Reformation zeal to
obliterate Roman Catholic
imagery, and years of neglect.
Finally, as a slum threatened with
demolition, it was saved to
become a museum in 1953. It
provides a faithful representation
of life for the comfortable
burghers of Aberdeen in the late
17th century.

✉ 45 Guestrow, off Broad Street
☎ 01224 641086 🕐 Mon–Sat 10–5,
Sun 1–4 ✋ Free 🍴 Café (£)

Satrosphere Science Centre

This is one of Scotland's two interactive exhibitions of science and technology and a great place in the North to take kids. There are no 'do not touch' signs here; visitors are encouraged to touch, look and feel. About 80 of the 150 exhibits and experiments are on display at any one time. You can find out about the geological formation of northeast Scotland, marvel at the industry and organization inside a beehive then compare it with a colony of ants, guess what the mystery sticky liquids are, test the speed of your reactions, experience the Satrosphere's very own black hole and much, much more. Fascinating for visitors of all ages, it may trigger a lifelong interest in science.
www.satrosphere.net

✉ The Tram Sheds, 179 Constitution Street ☎ 01224 640340
🕐 Daily 10–5 ✋ Moderate

Tolbooth Museum

The Tolbooth Museum, within the granite Town House, was the town gaol in 17th-century Aberdeen. The claustrophobic narrow staircases and cramped cells chillingly evoke the grim existence of prisoners here. An audiovisual display and a lifelike model of a prisoner tell tales of the wretched life and of escapes from the bleak conditions.

✉ Castle Street ☎ 01224 621167/01569 766073 🕐 Jul to mid-Sep Tue–Sat 10–12:30, 1:30–5, Sun 12:30–3:30 ✋ Free

The North

BALLATER AND BALMORAL

Balmoral, a fine example of Scottish Baronial architecture, was converted to a private residence for Queen Victoria in 1855 and became a well-loved

summer residence for the Royal Family. The local shops in Ballater flaunt their 'By Royal Appointment' signs. The town is a grand base for exploring the area, and Balmoral Estate hires out ponies for pony trekking.

✚ 9E ✉ Balmoral Estate: 13km (8 miles) west of Ballater on the A93 ☎ 013397 42534; www.balmoralcastle.com ◷ Apr–Jul daily 10–5. Winter gardens by reserved guided tour only ♿ Moderate 🍴 Café (£)

BETTYHILL

This tiny coastal village, at the heart of the crofting community, suffered mass emigration during the Highland Clearances. Tiny **Strathnaver Museum** tells the story of some of the most horrific evictions, ordered by the Countess of Sutherland. Ironically the village was named after her. Nearby are two of the whitest sand beaches in Britain and the Invernaver Nature Reserve, where otters and Arctic terns can often be spotted.

🔁 7A

Strathnaver Museum

✉ Clachan, Bettyhill ☎ 01641 521418; www.strathnavermuseum.org.uk 🕓 Apr–Oct Mon–Sat 10–5, 2–5 (and by arrangement) 🖐 Inexpensive

THE CAIRNGORMS

Within the area of this range of mountains, outdoor enthusiasts can find skiing, canoeing, mountaineering, bicycling and walking and a rich variety of flora and fauna. The 40km (25 miles) of the Lairig Ghru, running through a majestic mountain pass from Aviemore to Braemar, are reputed to be the best walk in Scotland, although its unpredictable weather and biting cold can test the endurance of the most experienced walker. However, there are shorter, less demanding walks in this glorious landscape. Aviemore village is ideal for exploring the area and its

numerous shops sell and rent equipment. Nearby Loch Morlich Watersports and the Scottish National Sports Council's Glenmore Lodge provide facilities and training.

✚ 8E

🅸 Grampian Road, Aviemore ☎ 01479 810930; www.cairngorms.co.uk

🅒 Mon–Fri 8–8, Sat 9–5:30, Sun 10–4

CALEDONIAN CANAL AND THE GREAT GLEN

One of Thomas Telford's greatest engineering achievements was the Caledonian Canal linking lochs Ness, Oich, Lochy and Linnhe from Inverness in the east to Fort William in the west. A slow boat through the Great Glen, watching the reflection of forest greenery or massed broom along the banks, is a tranquil and awesome experience. For the more energetic there are lots of off-road walking or bicycling trails on disused military roads, the old rail line or the towpath. At Fort Augustus, **The Clansman Centre** illustrates 17th-century clan life in a reconstructed turf house.

✚ 6–7E

The Clansman Centre

✉ Canal bank, Fort Augustus ☎ 01320 366444; www.scottish-swords.com

🅒 Apr–Oct daily 10–6:30 💷 Inexpensive

CROMARTY

Cromarty is a picturesque village on the northeast
coast of the Black Isle. The local museum in the
old **courthouse** and the thatched cottage of Hugh
Miller's birthplace bring the varied past of this little
port to life. Take a boat trip to watch dolphins, porpoises and the
occasional killer whale. The massive oil rigs of Nigg and Invergordon
dominate the Cromarty Firth by day and light up the night.

🚩 8C

Cromarty Courthouse

✉ Church Street ☎ 01381 600418; www.cromarty-courthouse.org.uk
🕐 May–Sep Sun–Thu 11–4 🎫 Free

CULLODEN BATTLEFIELD

Best places to see, ➤ 40–41.

DORNOCH

In 1722, Dornoch was the last place in Scotland to burn a witch.
To the south of the town square, the Witch's Stone is a reminder of
the poor soul who was roasted in a barrel of tar for allegedly turning
her daughter into a pony. The focal point of the square is the tiny
cathedral. All but destroyed in the 16th century and rebuilt in the
19th century, it houses an eerie collection of skulls and coffins.

🚩 8C ℹ The Square ☎ 01862 810594 🕐 All year

FORT GEORGE

After the rout of Bonnie Prince Charlie's Highland army at Culloden in
1746, the Hanoverians embarked on a drastic plan to subdue the
'rebellious Scots'. One measure was the construction of Fort George,
on a spit running into the Moray Firth. It is still an army barracks and
home of the Regimental Museum of the Queen's Own Highlanders.

🚩 8D ✉ Ardersier, B9039, off the A96 west of Nairn ☎ 01667 462777;
www.historic-scotland.gov.uk 🕐 Apr–Sep daily 9:30–6; Oct–Mar Mon–Sat
9:30–4:30, Sun 9:30–6:30 🎫 Moderate 🍴 Tea room (£)

FORT WILLIAM

Fort William's location, at the foot of the Great Glen and with the bulk of Ben Nevis to the east, makes it a popular area for walkers and mountaineers. It marks the end of the West Highland Way, which runs for 153km (95 miles) from the outskirts of Glasgow to Fort William. This is the most popular long-distance walk in Scotland and is broken down into seven daily sections; the final stretch brings you into Fort William with its pubs and restaurants.

The **Nevis Range Mountain Experience,** north of Fort William, offers a lift most of the way up the slopes of Aonach Mor (a neighbour of Ben Nevis) in a gondola. The 650-metre (2,133ft) trip is popular with climbers, walkers, cyclists and, if the weather is right, skiers.

➕ 6F 🛈 Cameron Centre, Cameron Square ☎ 01397 703781

Nevis Range Mountain Experience

✉ Off A82, 7 miles north of Fort William ☎ 01397 701801; www.nevisrange.co.uk 🕑 Jul, Aug daily 9:30–6; May–Jun, Sep–Nov 10–5; Dec–Apr 9–5 💷 Expensive

GLEN AFFRIC

As well as having some of the most serious walking, Glen Affric is undoubtedly one of the most beautiful glens in Scotland, with stretches of lovely lochs and forestry. The abundance of birch, pine and alder which grace the glen is a glorious sight in blazing autumn hues. It has one of the most remote youth hostels in Britain, requiring a hike of several miles to reach it.

🖶 6E ⊠ Southwest of Cannich, off the A831

GLEN COE

Best places to see, ➤ 44–45.

INVEREWE GARDEN

The Gulf Stream flows around the west coast of Scotland producing a warm temperate climate, ideal for gardens. Inverewe was created between 1862 and 1922 by the estate owner,

Osgood Mackenzie. The garden has spilled out from its original walled enclave to cover the peninsula. Scots pine, birch, oak and rowan stand alongside semi-tropical exotic plants in a series of small gardens.

✚ 5C ✉ Poolewe ☎ 01445 781200; www.nts.org.uk 🕓 Easter–Oct daily 9–9; rest of year 9:30–5 ✋ Expensive 🍴 Restaurant (£)

INVERNESS

Inverness is an attractive town, built mainly in the 19th century, with a fine cathedral and castle. Situated on the Moray Firth at the eastern end of the Caledonian Canal, it is the largest town in the Highlands, a transport hub and the best base for exploring.

✚ 7D

ℹ Castle Wynd ☎ 01463 234353 🕓 All year

KINGUSSIE

Kingussie, a typical small town built around a single main street, is an oasis of tranquillity bypassed by the hurly-burly of the main artery north, the A9. At the **Highland Folk Museum** you can explore reconstructions of a Lewis black house (a traditional Hebridean low stone dwelling with thatched roof), a salmon smoking shed and a water mill, as well as finding out everything there is to know about the history of the area. Nearby the ruins of Ruthven Barracks stand proud and roofless against the skyline. They were part of the fortifications built to ensure stability in the region after the Jacobite Rebellion of 1745. From Ruthven you can walk a surviving stretch of General Wade's military road, crossing a perfectly preserved example of a Wade bridge near Dalwhinnie.

✚ 8E

Highland Folk Museum

✉ Duke Street ☎ 01540 673551 🕓 Apr–Aug Mon–Sun 10:30–5:30; Sep–Oct Mon–Fri 9:30–4:30; Nov–Mar groups by appointment ✋ Moderate

LOCH NESS

The world-famous loch is forever linked to its resident beastie, the Loch Ness Monster. The loch is long and deep and swarming with Nessie spotters. At Drumnadrochit there are two monster exhibitions: the Original Loch Ness Monster Exhibition, and the considerably better **Loch Ness 2000 Exhibition Centre.**

Castle Urquhart, a couple of miles south, is the best monster spotting site, where most of the Nessie photographs have been taken. The ruins of the 14th-century castle themselves are worth a visit. Perched atop a rocky cliff the castle was of strategic importance in guarding the Great Glen. It was destroyed in 1692 to prevent its use by the Jacobites.

✚ 7D

Loch Ness 2000 Exhibition Centre

✉ Drumnadrochit ☎ 01456 450573; www.loch-ness-scotland.com
🕐 Jul–Aug daily 9–6:30, Jun and Sep 9–6, Feb–May and Oct 9:30–5, Nov–Jan 9:30–3:30 ✋ Moderate

ROTHIEMURCHUS

The huge estate of Rothiemurchus, belonging to the Grant family, extends from the village of Aviemore to the Cairngorm plateau. The lovely woodlands here, with the Cairngorms forming a backdrop, are particularly noted for their magnificent Caledonian pine. From the estate visitor centre, there's access to a superb mountain bicycle track and miles of footpaths through forests, over heather moorlands and by lochs and rivers. There is also a nature trail around Loch an Eilean and other activities include clay-pigeon shooting, ranger walks and fishing on the Spey.

✚ 8E

www.rothiemurchus.net

✉ 1.5km (1 mile) southeast from Aviemore on the Ski Road ☎ 01479 812345

🕙 Daily 9:30–5:30 ✋ Free; various charges for different activities

🍴 Restaurant, coffee shop (£–££)

SHETLAND AND ORKNEY

These islands were formerly Norwegian, and the Norse influence is evident in language and customs. Orkney is a few miles off the mainland, while Shetland is 96km (60 miles) further north. Each one is a scattering of islands, abounding in wildlife, particularly sea birds. In both, the Mainland refers to the main island while the rest of Scotland is known as 'The Sooth'.

🛈 Shetland Island Tourism, Market Cross, Lerwick ☎ 01595 693434; www.visitshetland.com 🛈 Orkney Tourist Board, 6 Broad Street, Kirkwall ☎ 01856 872001; www.visitorkney.com

SHETLAND
Foula

About 22km (14 miles) east of the Mainland is Foula. Traces of an ancient way of life – peat fires and eking out a living – cling to this remote island. Until a few years ago, the island schoolteacher was responsible for christenings, marriages and funerals in his role as Church of Scotland missionary. Foula teems with birds, particularly puffins and great skuas.

✚ 27P 🚢 Ferries to Foula from Walls ☎ 07881 823732 for times

Jarlshof

This ancient settlement was inhabited from the Stone Age to the 17th century. There's a broch (round tower of two layers of stones with stairs built into the thickness of the wall) and a medieval building, but the most interesting dwellings are the Norse longhouses and the complex wheelhouse structures with underground corridors, bedrooms and central hearths.

✚ 28Q 🖂 Sumburgh ☎ 01950 460112 🕓 Apr–Sep daily 9:30–6:30 ✋ Inexpensive

Lerwick

On Lerwick's attractive waterfront fishing boats jostle along-side oil industry transporters and the Greenpeace *Rainbow*

Warrior, a frequent visitor. The narrow main street runs behind the harbour and countless tiny alleys climb up the hill.

Up Helly Aa, once a pagan fire festival to celebrate the end of the ancient Yule celebration, is now a well-organized spectacle in which a thousand men with blazing torches march through the streets of Lerwick. Behind them they drag a Viking galley to the burning ground where they throw their torches into the vessel. If you can't be there to see it in January there is an excellent exhibition with an audiovisual with examples of Viking costumes and pictures of bearded warriors in winged helmets, standing before the burning craft.

✛ 28P

Up Helly Aa Exhibition

✉ Galley Shed, off Sunniva Street ⏱ Mid-May to mid-Sep Tue, Fri and Sat 2–4, 7–9 💷 Inexpensive

ORKNEY
Italian Chapel
Although built from Nissen huts, concrete, barbed wire and paint by Italian POWs in 1943, the love and reverence which went into this exquisite little gem are evident. Artist Domenico Chiocchetti designed the interior, creating *trompe-l'oeil* stonework and windows, and a magnificent fresco altarpiece.

✚ 26S ✉ Lamb Holm ⏱ Apr–Sep daily 9am–10pm; Oct–Mar 9–4:30
👆 Free; donations welcomed

Kirkwall and St Magnus Cathedral
Kirkwall is the largest town in Orkney and the island capital. St Magnus Cathedral, founded in 1137 and built over a period of 300 years, has architectural details from Norman to early Gothic. The exquisite carving, the red and yellow stone and its small size give it a feeling of delicacy and lightness for a medieval cathedral.

✚ 26S ✉ Kirkwall

Maes Howe
This neolithic burial chamber is the finest chambered tomb in Western Europe. You creep through a long narrow stone tunnel to reach the central chamber. It was built 4,000 years ago with such precision that the sun lights the tunnel at sunset on midwinter. No treasures were found inside: Vikings had beaten the Victorians to the plunder.

✚ 25S ✉ Stenness ☎ 01856 761606 ⏱ Apr–Sep daily 9:50–5:30; Oct–Mar Mon–Sat 9:30–4:30, Sun 2–4:30. Tours only: timed ticketing operates, must be pre-booked 👆 Moderate 🍴 Café (£)

Skara Brae
Best places to see, ▶ 50–51.

around Shetland, Mousa Island and Broch

Mousa is a small, uninhabited island to the east of Mainland Shetland, with an unrivalled example of a broch – the circular, fortified, drystone tower of the Iron Age. Abundant wildlife includes seals and storm petrels, eider ducks, waders and skuas, which swoop and dive everywhere, unworried by the approach of humans.

Turn right from the jetty and follow the path along the coast to your right until you come to the broch.

Built between 100BC and AD100, Mousa Broch, featured in the great Viking Sagas, remains almost intact. A narrow passage leads to an inner courtyard where the encircling massive stone wall bears in on you as you look up at the circle of sky 12m (39ft) above. Torches are supplied to climb the narrow, worn stairs in the dark space within the walls. At the top you can see where great beams would have supported the turf roof and view a coastline that the original builders would still recognize.

Follow the path around the coast from the broch or head inland with the remains of a house on your right.

The map you get from the boatman indicates areas to be avoided during the nesting season. Either way you will reach two sheltered bays on the east side where seals gather. There may be just two or three swimming or possibly a hundred or so in and out of the water.

From the bay follow the path back to the jetty and the small stone cottage that now serves as a shepherd's hut.

Distance 6km (4 miles) **Time** 3 hours (including ferry)
Start/end point The pier at Leebitton Harbour, Sandwick ☎ 01590 431367 (ferryman) ✚ 28Q
Lunch There are no facilities on Mousa, so take a packed lunch

SKYE AND THE WESTERN ISLES

This group of islands contain some of the bleakest and most beautiful scenery in Scotland. From the majestic Cuillins of Skye through the flat waterlogged moors of North Uist and the rolling hills of Harris to the timeless charm of the smaller islands, Eigg, Muck, Rum, Canna, Barra and Eriskay, you could spend a lifetime exploring here. Walk the ancient paths and hill tracks, seek out secluded bays or visit prehistoric settlements and still there are further delights to uncover.

Western Isles Tourist Board, 26 Cromwell Street, Stornoway, Isle of Lewis 01851 703088; www.visitthehebrides.com

Callanish Stones, Isle of Lewis

Built over 4,000 years ago, and 1,000 years before the pyramids of Egypt, this is possibly the most spectacular and intact prehistoric site in Europe. Standing on a raised site, the stones are 4.5m (15ft) high and form the shape of a Celtic cross.The main part of the site is a circle of 13 stones with an avenue of 19 monoliths leading north.

3B Callanish 01851 621422; www.callanishvisitorcentre.co.uk

⊕ Visitor centre Apr–Sep Mon–Sat 10–6; Oct–Mar Wed–Sat 10–4. Stones always open 🖐 Visitor centre inexpensive; no charge to view stones 🍴 Café (£)

Lewis Loom Centre, Stornoway, Isle of Lewis

Harris tweed production is one of the mainstays of the local economy in the Outer Hebrides and is still woven by hand. The only place in the islands where the entire production process can be seen is the Lewis Loom Centre in Stornoway, where Ronnie Mackenzie has set up a small museum and exhibition display. Ronnie will demonstrate carding, spinning and warping, and explain about natural and synthetic dyes. Then he'll weave some cloth, talk about waulking the finished material and answer questions. His shop stocks a wide variety of Harris tweed clothing.

✚ 4B ✉ Old Grainstore, 3 Bayhead Street, Stornoway ☎ 01851 704500 ⊕ Apr–Dec Mon–Sat 9–6 🖐 Inexpensive

Raasay Outdoor Centre, Raasay

Raasay is the place for adventure sports. This outdoor venue provides equipment and instruction for a wide array of activities including sailing, water-skiing, sailboarding, mountain bicycling, walking and climbing. Accommodation is in the house where Dr Samuel Johnstone (1709–84), a leading journalist and literary figure, and his biographer, James Boswell (1704–95), lodged during their tour of the Hebrides. The activities are open to day visitors, too.

www.raasay-house.co.uk

✚ 4D ✉ Raasay House, Inverarish ☎ 01478 660266 ⊕ Accommodation all year, activities Easter–Oct 🖐 Expensive

Skye Museum of Island Life, Isle of Skye

This 'living museum' is a series of seven thatched black houses, reconstructed to form an ancient island township. The original black house on the site looks much as it did when it was last inhabited in the late 1950s. Here locals re-create the crofting way of life as it was a century ago. Behind the museum is the grave of Flora MacDonald who helped Bonnie Prince Charlie to escape the Hanoverian forces after his defeat at Culloden.

➕ 4C ✉ Kilmuir, near Loch Ainort ☎ 01470 552206 🕐 Easter to mid-Oct Mon–Sat 9:30–5 🍴 Tea machine ♿ Inexpensive

ULLAPOOL

Ullapool, at the head of Loch Broom, was built as a planned fishing village in 1788 by the British Fisheries Society. Today, it is still a bustling fishing port, as well as the ferry terminal for the Western Isles and the main base for exploring Wester Ross. It has a lively venue at the Ceilidh Place (➤ 179), where people can enjoy the outdoors by day and sample live traditional music and dancing in the evening. The surrounding countryside abounds in walks such as the old drove road to Loch Achall and back over the summit of Meall Mor, with a breathtaking view over Loch Broom and the Summer Isles.

The Summer Isles are a small group of uninhabited islands accessible by boat from Ullapool and Achiltibuie during the summer months. Most trips allow an hour on shore on Tanera Mhor, the largest island in the group. As well as sea birds, you are likely to see seals, dolphins and porpoises. Five kilometres (3 miles) from Ullapool on Loch Broom, you will find **Leckmelm Shrubbery and Arboretum,** dating from the 1870s, which is renowned for its rare trees and plants, including rhododendrons and azaleas.

Corrieshalloch Gorge, on the A835 south of Ullapool, is a 1.5km (1-mile) long, 60m (197ft) deep box canyon with an information board which tells you all about its geological and botanical interest. However, it is the Falls of Measach that most people come to see. The 45m (148ft) cascade can be viewed from a narrow suspension bridge that spans the gorge or from the observation platform.

www.ullapool.co.uk

✚ 6C

ℹ 20 Argyle Street

☎ 01854 612486

🕐 Easter–Nov Mon–Fri 8–8, Sat 9–5:30, Sun 10–4

Leckmelm Shrubbery and Arboretum

✉ 5km (3 miles) south of Ullapool on A835

☎ No phone; www.gardensofscotland. org 🕐 Easter–Sep daily 10–6 🖐 Inexpensive

a drive around Harris and Lewis

This coastal drive around the islands of Lewis and Harris takes in the most important attractions in the Hebrides.

From Stornoway take the A859 towards Tarbert which is 56km (35 miles) away on Harris. Continue on the A859 to Leverburgh. From Leverburgh continue on the A859 as far as Rodel, then follow the local road as it meanders along the east coast via Manish to rejoin the A859 south of Tarbert.

Called the Golden Highway, because of the expense of building it, this is a winding, single-lane road with passing places. It connects a number of small remote settlements strung out across a land which resembles a moonscape – rugged, rocky, empty and painfully beautiful.

From Tarbert drive back towards Stornoway on the A859. At Leurbost, turn left on the local road which links with the A858 at Achmore. Follow this road to Callanish.

The standing stones of Callanish (► 172–173), constructed about a thousand years before the pyramids, stand above Loch Roag.

Continue on the road past Carloway, Arnol and through Barvas to Lional, then follow the signs for the Butt of Lewis.

Carloway Broch is worth a visit, and the nearby village of Garenin with its restored black houses should not be missed. Arnol Black House was built in 1885 and served continuously as a dwelling until 1964. The young woman who lived there with her mother is now the caretaker and guide.

From the lighthouse at the Butt of Lewis return by the same route as far as Barvas then turn left on to the A857 to Stornoway.

Distance 298km (185 miles)
Time 6–8 hours depending on stops
Start/end point Stornoway ✚ 4B
Lunch Harris Hotel (££) ✉ Tarbert ☎ 01859 502154

HOTELS

ABERDEEN
Aberdeen Douglas (££–£££)
This traditional city-centre hotel has every facility and good spacious bedrooms. Good weekend break offers.
✉ 43–45 Market Street ☎ 01224 582255; www.aberdeendouglas.com

BALLATER
Glen Lui Hotel (££)
This medium-sized hotel offers well-equipped rooms, a pleasant garden and a good restaurant that uses local, seasonal produce.
✉ Invercauld Road ☎ 013397 55402; www.glen-lui-hotel.co.uk

INVERNESS
The Waterside Hotel (££)
Set beside the River Ness and a few minutes' walk from the town centre, this pretty hotel offers good rooms at keen prices.
✉ 19 Ness Bank ☎ 01463 233065; www.thewatersideinverness.co.uk

KIRKWALL, ORKNEY
Ayre Hotel (££)
Relaxed seafront hotel offering the best of local ingredients in its superb restaurant. The Saturday night folk sessions feature some of Orkney's most talented musicians.
✉ Ayre Road ☎ 01856 873001; www.ayrehotel.co.uk

LERWICK, SHETLAND
Glen Orchy House (££)
A conversion from a convent building. Awesome breakfasts and Thai food in the restaurant. This is the best place on the islands.
✉ 20 Knab Road ☎ 01595 692031; www.guesthouselerwick.com

MUIR OF ORD
The Dower House (££)
Early 18th-century building in secluded gardens. Well placed for Royal Dornoch, and other golf courses, and as a touring base.
✉ Highfield ☎ 01463 870090; www.thedowerhouse.co.uk

ONICH

The Onich Hotel (££)

A beautifully situated waterside hotel with fabulous views, large, comfortable bedrooms, good local food and a friendly welcome.

✉ Onich ☎ 01855 821214; www.onich-fortwilliam.co.uk

STORNOWAY, ISLE OF LEWIS

Cabarfeidh (££)

Friendly hotel with locally sourced food. A good base from which to explore the Western Isles.

✉ On the edge of town ☎ 01851 702604; www.cabarfeidh-hotel.co.uk

ULLAPOOL

The Ceilidh Place (£–££)

Warm, friendly, intimate and probably the best place to stay while exploring the Western Highlands. As well as superb Scottish food in the coffee shop or the more formal restaurant, the Ceilidh Place has its own book shop and budget accommodation in the adjacent clubhouse. A great place to hear folk music (➤ 71).

✉ West Argyll Street ☎ 01854 612103; www.theceilidhplace.com

RESTAURANTS

ABERDEEN

Café 52 (£)

This tiny bistro is woth seeking out for its atmosphere, outside summer eating and dishes such as Tamworth pork loin.

✉ The Green ☎ 01224 590094; www.cafe52.net

The Foyer (££)

This buzzing restaurant serves excellent modern Scottish cooking in sleek surroundings – and the profits go to a homeless charity.

✉ 82A Crown Street ☎ 01224 582277

The Square (£–££)

The look is contemporary and so is the menu at this popular and relaxed central restaurant, much-liked by young Aberdonians.

✉ 1 Golden Square ☎ 01224 646362

BALLATER
Darroch Learg Hotel (£££)

A sophisticated menu in the attractive dining room of this 19th-century country house perched high above the village. Locally sourced game and excellent seafood dishes are available and there is an interesting 7-course tasting dinner.

✉ Braemar Road ☎ 01339 755443

Green Inn (££)

An innovative selection of modern Scottish dishes such as seared fillet of Scotttish beef with smoked *pomme purée* and caramelized shallots served by chef Chris O'Halloran, son of proprietor, Trevor.

✉ 9 Victoria Road ☎ 01339 755701

DUFFTOWN
Taste of Speyside (£)

Scottish right down its tartan carpet, with a menu including Cullen skink (► 12), traditional clootie dumpling topped with Glenfiddich liqueur and a host of local delicacies such as smoked venison. Finish with a glass of malt bearing the same name as the street.

✉ 10 Balvenie Street ☎ 01340 820860

FORT WILLIAM
Crannog Restaurant (££)

Converted from an old fisherman's gear shed, this restaurant, the best in Fort William, sits out on the pier. Naturally they serve seafood, mostly local.

✉ Town Pier ☎ 01397 705589; www.crannog.net

GLAMIS
Castleton House Hotel (££)

Country house with 700-year-old moat. Try the fine whisky fruit tart, preceded perhaps by langoustine cappuccino followed by cod and crab fishcake on a dressing of mixed beans. Main dishes could be fillet of Scotch Beef with buttered spinach, dauphinoise potatoes and a red wine sauce.

✉ Forfar ☎ 01307 840340; www.castletonglamis.co.uk

INVERNESS
Café 1 (£)
French bistro classics meet contemporary British. Try liver and bacon with an onion marmalade and potatoes and parsnip mash followed by a selection of French and Scottish cheeses.
✉ 76 Castle Street ☎ 01463 226200; www.cafe1.net

Rocpool (££–£££)
Inverness's most stylish restaurant features Mediterranean and Scottish cooking in its reasonably priced lunchtime menus and more expensive – and eclectic – evening offerings.
✉ 1 Ness Walk ☎ 01463 717274; www.rocpoolrestaurant.com

KINGUSSIE
The Cross (£££)
Katie and David Young are the friendly proprietors of this former tweed mill, now a restaurant with accommodation. Fresh local and seasonal produce is cooked in a deceptively simple manner and served caringly but with the minimum of fuss. Excellent wine list.
✉ Tweed Mill Brae, Ardbroilach Road ☎ 01540 661166

LERWICK
Monty's (£–££)
See page 59.

PLOCKTON
The Seafood Restaurant (££)
The seafood platter is the star turn at this good eating place, which also offers home-smoked fish, prawns and crab and local beef.
✉ Innes Street ☎ 01599 544 222; www.plocktoninn.co.uk

PORTREE, ISLE OF SKYE
Cuillin Hills Hotel (££)
Views of the Cuillins over Portree Bay are the highlight of an evening here. Built in 1870 as a hunting lodge, it is now one of the premier eating places on Skye.
✉ Just north of Portree off the A855 ☎ 01478 612003

SHIELDAIG
Tigh an Eilean Hotel (££)
Scotland is full of splendid restaurants. This one is a corker. The cooking is simple and uses fresh, quality produce. Try the crab dijonnaise, grilled lamb cutlets or poached salmon hollandaise.

✉ Off the A896 ☎ 01520 755251; www.stevecarter.com/hotel

TORRIDON
Loch Torridon Hotel (£££)
This hotel is in a great location overlooking the excruciatingly beautiful Loch Torridon. Try the lobster with cucumber spaghetti in a lobster and sherry sauce, or deer fillet with juniper and sweated red onions.

✉ Off the A896, southwest of Kinlochewe ☎ 01445 791242

ULLAPOOL
The Ceilidh Place (££)
See page 58.

SHOPPING

TWEEDS, TARTANS AND WOOLLIES
Johnston's Cashmere Centre
This combined shop and visitor centre tells the story of cashmere then gives you the chance to shop amid the mouth-watering selection of finest cashmere clothes and accessories.

✉ Newmill, Elgin ☎ 01343 554099; www.johnstonscashmere.com

CRAFTS AND GIFT SHOPS
Highland Stoneware
Hand-painted pottery and stoneware with an enormous selection of table- and cookware, as well as the more decorative gift items.

✉ Mill Street, Ullapool ☎ 01854 612980; www.highlandstoneware.com

WHISKY
The Whisky Shop
Stock up here from a wide selection of local whiskies.

✉ 1 Fife Street, Dufftown ☎ 01340 821097

Highland Park Distillery
The Orcadian version of 'The Water of Life'.
✉ Kirkwall, Orkney ☎ 01856 874619; www.highlandpark.co.uk

FOOD
Walkers Shortbread
Famous tartan shortbread is made here. Buy it from the factory shop as well as oatcakes, cakes and other biscuits.
✉ Aberlour, Aberlour on Spey ☎ 01340 871555;
www.walkersshortbread.com

Baxters
This is the place to buy Mrs Baxter's celebrated products. There's a full range of soups, jams and preserves, along with great gift ideas in the Cookshop. There is a self-service restaurant.
✉ Baxters Visitor Centre, Fochabers ☎ 01343 820666;
www.baxters.com

ENTERTAINMENT

Aquadome
Flumes and a wave machine make this pool a must for kids on a rainy day. For serious swimmers there's a competition pool and the usual health facilities, including massage and hydrotherapy.
✉ Bught Park, Inverness ☎ 01463 667500

The Ceilidh Place
See page 71.

Eden Court Theatre
The main venue in the Highlands for drama, music and dance.
✉ Bishops Road, Inverness ☎ 01463 234234; www.eden-court.co.uk

Hootananny
See page 71.

The Seaforth
See page 71.

Index

Acknowledgements

The Automobile Association would like to thank the following photographers, companies and picture libraries for their assistance in the preparation of this book.

Abbreviations for the picture credits are as follows – (t) top; (b) bottom; (c) centre; (l) left; (r) right; (AA) AA World Travel Library.

4l Cuillin Hills, AA/S Whitehorne; **4c** Glenfinnan viaduct, AA/S Day; **4r** Glen Coe, AA/P Sharpe; **5l** View from Calton Hill, AA/K Paterson; **5r** Kilchurn Castle, AA/J Carnie; **6/7** Cuillin Hils, AA/S Whitehorne; **8/9** Tobermory, AA/R Eames; **10bl** Highland Cow, AA/S Day; **10br** Iona, AA/R Eames; **10cr** Edinburgh Castle, AA/J Smith; **10/1t** Cairngorms, AA/J Smith; **10/1b** Tartan ties, AA/K Paterson; **11cl** Brodick Castle, AA/K Paterson; **12** Seafood, AA/E Ellington; **12/3t** Salmon, Photodisc; **12/3b** Haggis, AA/J Henderson; **13** Mustard, AA/J Carnie; **14/5** Whisky, AA/J Smith; **15tr** Shortbread, AA/K Paterson; **15br** Edinburgh rock, AA/K Paterson; **16t** Barras, AA/M Alexander; **16/7b** Barrels, AA/E Ellington; **17tl** Museum of Scotland, AA/K Paterson; **17br** Haggis, AA/K Paterson; **18** Edinburgh Castle, AA/J Smith; **18/9** Goat Fell, AA/ J Carnie; **19** Jedburg Abbey, AA/S Anderson; **20/1** Glenfinnan Viaduct, AA/S Day; **25** Edinburgh festival, AA/K Paterson; **26** Forth rail bridge, AA/J Smith; **27** Information Centre, AA/S Whitehorne; **28** Tour bus, AA/J Smith; **29** Taxi, AA/J Smith; **32** Policemen, AA/K Paterson; **34/5** Glen Coe, AA/P Sharpe; **36** Alloway, AA/S Anderson; **36/7** Kirk Alloway, AA/K Paterson; **38/9t** Burrell Collection, AA/S Whitehorne; **38/9b** Burrell Collection, AA/R Elliot; **39** Burrell Collection, AA/S Whitehorne; **40** Culloden Moor, AA/S Anderson; **40/1** Culloden Moor, AA/S Anderson; **42** Stained glass in St Margaret's Chapel, AA/J Smith; **42/3t** Edinburgh Castle, AA/D Corrance; **42/3b** Military Tatoo, AA/J Smith; **44** Glen Coe, AA/S Anderson; **45** Piper, AA/S Anderson; **44/5** Glen Coe, AA/S Anderson; **46t** New Lanark, AA/S Whitehorne; **46b** New Lanark, AA/M Taylor; **46/7** New Lanark, AA/S Gibson; **48** Rosslyn Chapel, AA/R Elliot; **48/9** Rosslyn Chapel, AA/M Alexander; **49t** Rosslyn Chapel, AA/M Alexander; **49b** Rosslyn Chapel, AA/M Alexander; **50/1** Skara Brae, AA/S Whitehorne; **51t** Skara Brae, AA/S Whitehorne; **551b** Skara Brae, AA/E Ellington; **52** The Tenement House, AA/S Gibson; **52/3t** The Tenement House, AA/S Gibson; **52/3b** The Tenement House, AA/S Gibson; **54** Traquair House, AA/K Paterson; **54/5t** Traquair House, AA/M Alexander; **54/5b** Traquair House, AA/S Anderson; **56/7** View of Edinburgh, AA/K Paterson; **58/9** Ceilidh Place hotel and restaurant, AA/R Elliot; **60/1** Golf, AA/J Carnie; **62/3** Climber on Ciste Dhubb, AA/R Elliot; **64** Greyfriars Bobby, AA/K Paterson; **64/5** Greyfriars churchyard, AA/D Corrance; **66** Glasgow Science Centre, AA/S Whitehorne; **68** Urquhart Castle, AA/J Smith; **71** Traditional music, AA/C Coe; **72/3** Kilchurn Castle, AA/J Carnie; **75** View from Scott monument, AA/J Smith; **76** View from Arthur's Seat, AA/D Corrance; **77** Calton Hill, Edinburgh Inspiring Capital, www.edinburgh-inspiringcapital.com; **78** Edinburgh Castle, AA/J Smith; **78/9** National Museum of Scotland, Edinburgh Inspiring Capital, www.edinburgh-inspiringcapital.com; 79 Palace of Holyroodhouse Abbey, AA/K Paterson; 80 Princes Street, D Noble/Alamy; 81 Canongate buildings, Edinburgh Inspiring Capital, www.edinburgh-inspiringcapital.com; **82/3** The Debating Chamber at the Scottish Parliament Complex in Edinburgh Adam Elder/Scottish Parliament; **83t** Abbotsford House, AA/M Alexander; **83b** Abbotsford House, AA/J Beazley; **84/5t** Haddington, AA/J Beazley; **84/5b** Mary Queen of Scots House, AA/S Anderson; **85** Jedburgh Abbey, AA/S & O Mathews; **86/7** Kelso, AA/S &O Mathews; **88** Gladstone Court Museum, AA/M Taylor; **90** St Abbs, AA/M Alexander; **101** Culzean Estate, AA/K Paterson; **102** Museum of Modern Art, AA/S Whitehorne; **102/3** Glasgow School of Art, AA/M Alexander; **103** Charles Rennie Mackintosh, AA/S Gibson; **104t** Holmwood House, AA/S Whitehorne; **104b** Kelvingrove Museum, AA/S Whitehorne; **104/5** Kelvingrove Museum, AA/S Whitehorne; **105** Museum of Transport, AA/M Alexander; **107** The Tall Ship at Glasgow Harbour, The Tall Ship at Glasgow Harbour; **109** Templeton's Carpet Factory, AA/S Whitehorne; **110** Isle of Arran, AA/K Paterson; **110/11** Culzean Castle, AA/S Anderson; **112** Globe Inn, AA/M Alexander; **112/3** Dumfries, AA/P Sharpe; **113** Galloway Forest Park, AA/H Williams; **114/5** Wigtown, AA/J Beazley; **115** New Abbey, AA; **117** Sweetheart Abbey, AA/D Hardley; **127** Dee Valley, AA/R Weir; **128/9** The Discovery, AA/J Smith; **129** Frigate Unicorn, AA/J Smith; **130/1t** McManus Gallery, AA/S Day; **130/1b** McManus Gallery, AA/S Day; **131** Verdant Works, AA/J Smith; **132** Lower Largo, AA/M Taylor; **132/3** Loch Leven, AA/S Day; **134/5** Braemar, AA/R Weir; **135t** Bo'ness and Kinneal Railway Station, AA/M Alexander; **135b** Culross, AA/J Smith; **136** Crail AA/M Taylor; **136/7** Hill House, AA/K Paterson; **138** Tobermory, AA; **138/9** Bullock, AA/J Carnie; **139** Inveraray, AA/S Whitehorne; **140/1** View from Ben Cruachan, AA/S Anderson; **142/3** Oban, AA/P Sharpe; **144** St Andrews, AA/J Smith; **144/5t** Pitlochry Highland Games, AA/S Day; **144/5b** St Andrews, AA/R Weir; **146/7** Wallace Monument in Stirling, AA/S Whitehorne; **147** The Trossachs, AA/A Baker; **153** Raasay from the Isle of Skye, AA/R Elliot; **154** Aberdeen harbour, AA/K Paterson; **155** Provost Skeen's House, AA/E Ellington; **156/7t** Ballater, AA/R Weir; **156/7b** Balmoral, AA/J Beazley; **158t** Bettyhill, AA/S Whitehorne; **158b** Cairngorms, AA/J Smith, **158/9** Neptune' Staircase, AA/S Day; **160/1t** Cromarty, AA/S Whitehorne; **160/1b** Fort William, AA/S Day; **162** Glen Affric, AA/J Henderson; **163** Inverewe Gardens, AA/Jeff Beazley; **164/5** Loch Ness, AA/J Smith; **166/7** Lerwick, AA/E Ellington; **168** Italian Chapel, Orkney, AA/S Whitehorne; **169** Maes Howe, AA/S Whitehorne; **170/1** Grey seal, AA/M Moody; **172/3** Callanish Stones, AA/R Elliot; **174** Skye museum of Island Life, AA/S Whitehorne; **174/5** Ullapool, AA/S Whitehorne; **176** Butt of Lewis, AA/R Eames; **177** Carloway Broch, AA/S Whitehorne.

Every effort has been made to trace the copyright holders, and we apologise in advance for any accidental errors. We would be happy to apply the corrections in the following edition of this publication.

Sight locator index

This index relates to the maps on the covers. We have given map references to the main sights of interest in the book. Grid references in italics indicate sights featured on town maps. Some sights within towns may not be plotted on the maps.

Questionnaire

Dear Traveler

Your comments, opinions and recommendations are very important to us.
So please help us to improve our travel guides by taking a few minutes to
complete this simple questionnaire.

Send to: Essential Guides,
MailStop 64, 1000 AAA Drive, Heathrow, FL 32746–5063

Your recommendations...

We always encourage readers' recommendations for restaurants, nightlife
or shopping – if your recommendation is added to the next edition of the
guide, we will send you a FREE AAA Essential Guide of your choice.
Please state below the establishment name, location and your reasons for
recommending it.

_____

_____

_____

_____

Please send me AAA Essential _____

About this guide...

Which title did you buy?

_____ **AAA Essential**

Where did you buy it? _____

When? m m / y y

Why did you choose a AAA Essential Guide? _____

_____

_____

Did this guide meet with your expectations?

Exceeded ☐   Met all ☐   Met most ☐   Fell below ☐

Please give your reasons _____

_____

_____

_____

continued on next page...

DAVID M. HUNT LIBRARY

63 MAIN ST.
P.O. BOX 217
FALLS VILLAGE, CT 06031-0217
860-824-7424

Were there any aspects of this guide that you particularly liked?

Is

C A R D

DATE DUE

			PRINTED IN U.S.A.

Thank you for taking the time to complete this questionnaire.

All information is for AAA internal use only and will not be distributed outside the organization to any third parties.